COMMUNITY DEVELOPMENT IN SOUTH AFRICA

A GUIDE FOR AMERICAN DONORS

D1445861

MICHAEL SINCLAIR

INVESTOR RESPONSIBILITY RESEARCH CENTER

The Investor Responsibility Research Center compiles and impartially analyzes information on the activities of business in society, on activities of institutional investors, on efforts to influence such activities, and on related public policies. IRRC's publications and other services are available by subscription or individually. IRRC's work is financed primarily by annual subscription fees paid by some 300 investing institutions for the Social Issues Service, Corporate Governance Service and South Africa Review Service. This report is a publication of the South Africa Review Service. The Center was founded in 1972 as an independent, not-for-profit corporation. It is governed by a 21-member board of directors, most of whom represent subscribing institutions.

Executive Director: Margaret Carroll.
South Africa Review Service Director: David Hauck.
Editor: Carolyn Mathiasen.

IRRC is grateful for the support of the
Ford Foundation in the preparation of this report.

TABLE OF CONTENTS

INTRODUCTION

The sharp increase in American concern over the situation in South Africa has led not only to louder calls for U.S. firms to pull out, but also to a greater allocation of funds by American foundations, universities, companies and the government to black community development projects in South Africa. While appreciative of American concern and thankful for the additional resources, South Africans nevertheless question how the money will be spent, and black South Africans in particular wonder if American donors have a political agenda that may conflict with their own.

Because many of the U.S. donors lack first-hand experience with South Africa, there often is confusion and uncertainty about where U.S. involvement is most appropriate and a glaring lack of awareness of the subtleties of black community politics that affect community development projects. One result is that a great deal of effort and money has been and will continue to be misdirected. Moreover, American-supported projects that champion certain economic and political values could elicit suspicion and rejection from the individuals and institutions in South Africa that American agencies aim to assist. Whether these funds will be used effectively to support undertakings that lay the groundwork for a politically stable and economically healthy South Africa after white domination has ended depends to a large extent on giving donors a clear idea of the social and political influences affecting community development.

Community development refers to all activities aimed at socio-economic advancement, cultivation of skills for self-reliance and acceleration of the process of political "empowerment" in the black community in South Africa. Community development projects abound in South Africa and are administered by myriad private community development agencies, each of which has its own organizational characteristics, and some of which are more effective in achieving their objectives than others.

These organizations operate not only within the constraints of the apartheid system, but also within the realities of black resistance to apartheid. The result is a complex set of social and political influences that includes not only the South African government, but also the diversity of black politics, and that constitutes a significant factor in the success or failure of community development efforts.

This report examines the central questions affecting community development in South Africa and, on the basis of extensive interviews with black South Africans involved in community development projects, the church, trade unions and political organizations, maps out an access route for American donors. Interviewees were selected for their standing in the black community as well as their insight into and experience with the problems of community development in South Africa.

Paradoxically, American agencies are the most active in the development field in South Africa and the most politically controversial. The principal reason is a historic lack of American political sensitivity and the perception among most black South Africans that Americans have a political agenda that is diametrically opposed to theirs.

South Africans need well-directed developmental and educational assistance to prepare the ground for a majority government and to enhance the prospect for future political stability. This report reflects black South African opinion that if American private or government agencies aspire to play a meaningful part in this process, a fundamental reorientation of American attitudes and preconceptions about South Africa generally and community development in particular is necessary. The first section sketches the principal political actors and recent political history and suggests ways in which American donor agencies may navigate these political complexities. The second and third parts examine the priorities for community development and black perceptions of the American role in supporting black advancement in South Africa, as well as the characteristic American attitudes and preconceptions that have turned many black South Africans against the United States. In the concluding chapter a number of model opportunities for American donors or prospective donors are discussed.

RESEARCH METHODOLOGY

This report was prepared in two stages. First, during May and June 1986 the author conducted personal interviews in South Africa with 76 individuals, 69 of whom are blacks and the remainder whites. Interviewees were selected on two criteria — institutional affiliation and personal experience of community development work. With few exceptions, the interviewees were not national leaders, but second and third tier organizers, community workers and professionals. The sample encompassed an institutional spectrum that included the following major groupings: the black trade union movement (Cosatu, Cusa and Azactu); the mainstream, black dominated churches (South African Council of Churches, the Southern African Catholic Bishops' Conference); major internal black political organizations (the United Democratic Front, Azapo and Inkatha); the liberation movements (the African National Congress and the Pan-Africanist Congress); youth groups (Azasm, Azanyu, Soyco); black professional and special interest associations (the Black Management Forum, the African Teachers Association of South Africa, National African Federated Chamber of Commerce, South African Black Social Workers Association); and black run community development organizations and other institutions committed to black advancement.

The interviews took the form of, on average, two-hour discussions structured around a standard set of issues:

I. Perceptions of the priorities for community development in South Africa;
   — the reasons for apportioning priority to particular areas;
   — discussion of each of the priorities and the key aspects of each priority;
   — identification of organizations perceived to be making an effective contribution to each of the priority areas;
   — the rural-urban nexus, the homelands, and regional variations;
   — the impact of state repression on community leadership and community development programs.

II. Discussion on gaining access to the community development network in South Africa;
   — the institutional framework and the role of politics in community development;
   — the political expectations that blacks have of community development;
   — personal experiences in the development field; and
   — projects that have worked or failed.

III. Black attitudes toward the United States and American participation in community development in South Africa;
   — black evaluation of American-sponsored community development programs;
   — identification of guidelines for American involvement.

The author, IRRC Senior Analyst Michael Sinclair, is a white South African who has nearly 10 years experience with black community development programs, initially in townships outside Pretoria, and from 1983 through 1985 as Director of the United States-South Africa Leader Exchange Program in Johannesburg. The author had thus established personal acquaintance with 71 of the interviewees over a number of years. This fact facilitated access to a significant cross-section of the black community, and also reduced the suspicion that often inhibits discussion with less familiar acquaintances. To encourage interviewees to be as frank as possible, all discussions were conducted on the basis of confidentiality, but anonymous statements and opinions were deliberately used to elicit reaction and possible counter arguments from other respondents.

The second stage in the preparation of this guide entailed compiling an initial draft and circulating it for critical comment to a select group of 26 South Africans, most of whom had been among the original interviewees, and 11 Americans chosen principally for their personal expertise in areas related to the substance of the report.

The author traveled to South Africa again in September 1986 to discuss the reaction of South Africans to the initial draft and to discuss their suggested revisions. The draft was subsequently revised to take account of the expert comment.

NOTE: The term black is used throughout this report to refer to all South Africans who are not white. African, colored (mixed race) or Asian is used only where it is necessary to make a technical distinction among the three black race groups.

The terms community development and community organization refer to activities and organizations that are principally concerned with advancing the interests of the black community, but not necessarily limited to a particular geographic area or one type of activity.

EXECUTIVE SUMMARY

South Africa's history of racial oppression and black political resistance has created a complex political situation that affects almost every dimension of South African society. Many well-intentioned community development initiatives have run aground on the complexities of South African politics, but this result is not inevitable. Although it is not possible to escape the political dimension, it is possible to gain acceptance among black South Africans through sensitivity to the political aspirations and social needs of blacks.

I. THE POLITICAL CONTEXT

Most community development initiatives are aimed at the social, economic and political disadvantages of black South Africans. However, the underlying cause of black disadvantage is fundamentally political — in that political decisions by white South Africans have blocked access by blacks to resources and opportunities — and blacks thus judge community development initiatives almost exclusively by their political relevance. Community development in South Africa is aimed not only at providing a base for community subsistence, but at empowering black South Africans to resist repression and to build the institutions that will form the foundation of a new socio-political order. Consequently, most community development organizations have political affiliations.

There are various pointers to navigating through the political complexities, but all are founded upon a single premise — credibility with black South Africans.

THE CONSULTATION PROCESS

The credibility of any community development initiative in the eyes of most black South Africans depends on the approval of leading black activist groups. This political endorsement is in turn dependent upon the extent to which blacks perceive that the initiative reflects black political aspirations and needs. The key to the legitimation and acceptability of any undertaking is an extensive process of consultation with recognized black leaders, as well as respected black political and community organizations.

This process is often time-consuming and cumbersome, but it is indispensable to the effectiveness and acceptability of any community development initiative. The consultation process is not to ratify a preconceived agenda, but more to mold a particular concept to meet the articulated requirements of black South Africans. To be effective, the consultation process requires a dispassionate ear, but also an astute understanding of the nuances of black politics and South African society.

The consultation process should be conducted at three levels, and although there is a great deal of overlap among individuals and organizations at all three levels, consultation at one level will not substitute for consultation at the others.

Public black leadership: The sanction of internationally recognized black activist leaders is important in building credibility and may be useful in gaining access to the network of less public black leadership and community groups.

The organizational level: There is a network of organizations through which the legitimacy of any initiative may be ratified. This network includes the major union federations — Cosatu, Cusa and Azactu; the church — the South African Council of Churches and the Southern African Catholic Bishops' Conference; and the two principal internal resistance movements — the United Democratic Front and the Azanian People's Organization. These organizations have a national following, and their cooperation is invaluable.

Grassroots: Although the first two levels of consultation provide an umbrella legitimacy and are essential in the trust building exercise, the ultimate test of acceptability is the participation of community based organizations. Because most of the black civic associations that exist in nearly every black township are an amalgam of smaller community groups, they reflect "grassroots" attitudes and thus are well placed to conduct consultations within local communities.

Persons interviewed for this report perceived the "internal and external struggle as a continuum," implying that the role of the external resistance movements in the consultation process is also important. At the same time, leaders of the African National Congress and the Pan-Africanist Congress take the position that there is no substitute for consultation with "the people" and credible internal organizations.

The question of what constitutes a credible community development organization is a matter of political perception. Some organizations are more politically acceptable to blacks than others. Black society is generally divided into two groups, those that are referred to as "collaborators" — namely, blacks who are viewed as part of the apartheid structure — and "activists" — those who actively oppose apartheid and seek a radical transformation of society. The collaborators, an increasingly isolated minority, include members of the homeland governments and black town councils. Cooperation with any of these institutions will automatically exclude support from other blacks. There is particular sensitivity among activist blacks to any association with Inkatha.

In addition, there are schisms between organizations that profess activist goals.

PROGRESSIVE VERSUS STATUS QUO

Put simply, the principal difference is between organizations that are perceived to be status quo oriented — even though their objectives might seem quite radical — and those that are perceived to be "progressive."

Progressive organizations are perceived to be contributing to the black struggle for the restructuring of South African society. Whether they have specifically political objectives or are non-political, they are judged largely by the extent to which blacks empathize with their objectives.

Among progressive organizations there are cleavages between those that follow a non-racial line and those that adhere to black consciousness principles. The difference between these two groups has translated into bitter rivalry within the black community, and often the initiatives of one group or the other become the focus of such rivalry. The perceptional difference often revolves more around personalities than policy or objectives.

Although it is possible to rise above this factionalism through careful planning and evenhanded consultation, it is not possible to avoid the broader black political struggle. A political choice has to be made.

MAKING A POLITICAL CHOICE

The implication is that association with "progressive" as opposed to "status quo" organizations, consultation with recognized activist leaders as opposed to collaborators, and the acceptance of "black terms" as against the imposition of preconceived plans reflects a choice for black political liberation. Undertakings that profess to be meeting the needs of blacks, but are not rooted in the black political struggle, will be dismissed as "papering over the cracks of apartheid," one person interviewed for this report told IRRC. Politically suspect initiatives are likely to be rejected at the outset. Once political aspersions have been cast on a particular undertaking it is virtually impossible to redeem political credibility.

II. PRIORITY AREAS FOR COMMUNITY DEVELOPMENT IN SOUTH AFRICA

Interviewees emphasized that priorities for community development are interrelated and thus one is not necessarily more important than the other. However, there is agreement that the priorities fall broadly into three areas — alleviating black poverty, assisting the victims of apartheid and preparing the ground for majority government.

Although the problems of black impoverishment and underdevelopment are obviously a function of the present political system, a future majority government will be hard pressed to meet the social and economic expectations of black South Africans. Most blacks have been led to believe that if apartheid were removed there would be an immediate change in their quality of life. Many black political leaders realize that this is far from reality, however, and express concern that the inability of a future government to deliver a short-term improvement in the lot of the average black will lead to further political instability and dissent.

A more sophisticated understanding of the factors influencing economic development is essential not only for alleviating black poverty, but also for enhancing the stability of a future majority government.

The principal factors shaping the pattern of economic development in South Africa are population growth and migration, access to scarce resources (particularly water), the state of the rural economy (particularly subsistence food production and land distribution), economic growth and employment creation.

All of these factors are interdependent — South Africa's population is growing at a rate faster than that at which the economy can provide employment; at the same time, natural population growth in, as well as the relocation of black people to, the homelands has led to chronic overcrowding in these areas. Overcrowding in turn has impoverished agricultural land and gravely depleted natural resources such as firewood, leading to the collapse of the subsistence rural economy. As a result, rural Africans increasingly depend upon the industrial/urban sector for subsistence. The implications are large scale unemployment, rural poverty and increasing urban migration, as well as increasing social and political tensions arising from the economy's incapacity to cope with the social and political demands made upon it. Indeed, a recent government report suggested that unless South Africa acted on these issues now, it would face large scale social unrest where political rights would be forgotten in the battle for food and water. There is evidence that this battle has already begun.

BLACK PERCEPTIONS OF THE PRIORITIES
FOR COMMUNITY DEVELOPMENT

Interviewees involved in community development work were critical of the piecemeal perspective of community development that concentrates on a particular area (such as housing or education), because these are popular and visible causes, without clear insight into the nature of black underdevelopment. Most of those interviewed expressed the opinion that community development programs often perpetuate dependence by failing to address the basic causes of the poverty cycle or to transfer the skills needed for self-reliance.

Interviewees raised the following considerations as influencing their perspective on the priorities for community development:

The 'holistic perspective': Community development should concentrate on addressing the fundamental causes of black deprivation rather than simply ameliorating the symptoms of deprivation within existing structures. Palliative efforts do not alter dependency and, therefore, are not likely to enjoy the political support of blacks.

Reinventing the wheel: The uncoordinated efforts of various community development organizations generally fail to produce a significant cumulative impact on the dependency cycle. Most interviewees believed that it would be most useful to facilitate collaborative efforts and to expand existing organizations, rather than create new ones.

Transfer of skills: Interviewees felt strongly that community development agencies fail to transfer their skills. The argument is that blacks must be given the skills to develop and carry on particular community initiatives themselves.

Multiplier effect: Because needs in South Africa far outstrip the available resources, it is important to base priorities for support on attaining the maximum benefit for the maximum number of people.

A sense of the long term: The problems of deprivation in South Africa will not be addressed in the short term. The implication of this is that a long term commitment is important to ensure the fulfillment of any community development initiative.

The homelands: Interviewees stressed the interrelatedness of urban and rural conditions and the need to address both dimensions of the problem. This view raises the politically sensitive question of working in the homelands. Interviewees were adamant that the homelands could not be excluded, but they warned against direct dealings with homeland governments.

Interviewees identified the priority areas for community development as follows:

Addressing black deprivation
Rural subsistence;
Education;
Job creation;
Urban housing.

Assisting the victims of apartheid
Humanitarian assistance;
Legal aid;
Victims of brutality.

Developing the institutions of a post-apartheid society
The alternative media;
Leadership groups.

Refugee programs

ORGANIZATIONAL NETWORK

Few black community development organizations have a national network. Moreover, there is little cooperation among various organizations with similar interests. Some of the reasons are fierce competition for financial resources, differing ideological and political perceptions, and the generally personalized nature of organizational leadership.

Most black community groups have little more than a basic administrative structure or capability, and it is often necessary for donors to channel resources to smaller community projects through administratively more sophisticated intermediary organizations. However, the existence of intermediary organizations is not a substitute for developing administrative and organizational skills in grassroots organizations. There are a number of nationally based organizations that can facilitate access to smaller regional networks and local groups:

The church;
Political organizations;
Trade unions;
Professional and special interest groups.

REGIONAL CONSIDERATIONS

Black impoverishment is undoubtedly more severe in some regions. The Free State and the Eastern Cape are areas where conditions for blacks are particularly harsh. Moreover, blacks are critical of the almost exclusive focus on the major metropolitan areas, and they accuse donors of doing what is easiest, not what is most necessary.

RELIABLE MANAGEMENT

Although choosing organizations with the appropriate political credentials is most important, this factor should not override the need to ensure appropriate organizational, management and accounting skills. Different criteria might be applied to various organizations, depending on their sophistication, but a general evaluation could include the following:

— does the organization have an audited or unaudited financial statement?
— does the organization have any full-time employees, and what are their qualifications?
— what is the organization's track record?
— what other sources of financial support does the organization have?

An integral part of any community development initiative ought to be the training of blacks to manage and develop the undertaking. The training of blacks in administrative and organizational skills is in itself an important contribution to community leadership.

WHAT RESOURCES ARE MOST NEEDED?

Most interviewees argued that a combination of resources — money, technical skills and equipment — are most needed. Financial assistance is obviously basic to any undertaking, but most of those interviewed emphasized the need to train blacks in the basic skills to enable them to develop and manage community development initiatives.

III. AMERICAN INVOLVEMENT IN COMMUNITY DEVELOPMENT IN SOUTH AFRICA

Growing American involvement in community development programs in South Africa and the promise of even greater involvement has increased the concern of black South Africans that much of the assistance is misdirected. The argument is that the focus of American assistance is biased toward support for the initiatives that most closely conform to American political and social preconceptions. As a result, the focus of many American supported initiatives conflicts with the goals of credible, black anti-apartheid organizations. This fact, in turn, makes it difficult for such organizations to be unequivocally associated with American institutions.

BLACK ATTITUDES TOWARD AMERICAN INVOLVEMENT

Attitudes toward American philanthropy in South Africa have become intertwined with black antipathy to the U.S. administration's policy of "constructive engagement" toward South Africa, and with demands by many black South Africans that multinational corporations pull out of South Africa.

Constructive engagement: Interviewees charged that "constructive engagement" is premised upon the appeasement of whites and completely ignores the attitudes and aspirations of blacks. Furthermore, black antipathy to "constructive engagement" is underscored by a general aversion to what many blacks see as international American imperialism. Consequently, a number of interviewees mentioned a policy of deliberate avoidance of American officials and noted extreme sensitivity among many black organizations to accepting funds linked to the U.S. government. Most interviewees agreed that passage by the U.S. Congress of a comprehensive packet of sanctions had not affected this position.

Disinvestment: There is a curious contradiction between the forceful calls for disinvestment on the one hand, and the equally forceful plea for American resources for community development on the other. Interviewees explained that disinvestment is intended as a political action, but blacks have never thought of disinvestment as absolving Americans of further involvement in South Africa. Blacks do not want to be abandoned to their fate, either now or after majority government is in place.

American social and political preconceptions: Almost without exception, interviewees expressed the opinion that Americans "don't listen." In addition, interviewees argued that parallels that many Americans draw between the American civil rights movement and the liberation struggle in South Africa are misleading. Furthermore, most interviewees expressed the opinion that American involvement in community development is motivated more by political goals than by humanitarian concerns. Many suggested that Americans are trying to choose the government they would like to see in South Africa.

GUIDELINES FOR AMERICAN INVOLVEMENT

Despite strong criticism of American attitudes and an underlying political suspicion of the United States on the part of black South Africans, no one suggested that American support for community development is not needed or should not be increased. On the contrary, interviewees pointed to the enormity of South Africa's development needs. Most spoke in terms of the needs of a majority government to secure political stability, but others spoke only in humanitarian terms.

When questioned about the apparent contradiction between virulent criticism of the United States and the quest for additional American resources, a number of interviewees explained that attitudes toward the United States are shaped by two conflicting perceptions. On one level there is the negative perception of America's world role as an imperialist superpower, but there is also a very high regard for the priority that the United States attaches to human rights. Thus, blacks are essentially appealing to the United States to respond to their plight from a humanitarian motivation; not only do they feel ideologically moved to condemn American global policy, but they are fearful that their own political ideals might be subverted by American imperialism.

There are a number of pointers that might facilitate American access to black community development.

The reason for getting involved: It is important for donors or prospective donors to be clear about the reasons for their interest in community development in South Africa. If the reason is primarily self-interest, such as assuaging divestment lobbyists, winning kudos from shareholders, quieting a restive student body or building a political platform, then there is strong prospect of a hostile reception from black South Africans. If, on the other hand, the reason is primarily a humanitarian concern, there are a number of factors that will confirm the sincerity of this commitment in the eyes of black South Africans:
— be guided by the needs and aspirations of black South Africans;
— allow blacks to manage the initiative from the outset;
— address the basic causes of black disadvantage;
— make a long term commitment;
— attempt to harness resources other than money, such as computer and agricultural equipment, training and technical expertise, to ensure the effectiveness and long term impact of the initiative.

Avoid the 'grand splash': One aspect of American involvement in community development in South Africa that is criticized most often is the pursuit of publicity. The American penchant for public relations confirms black suspicions that Americans are motivated mostly by self-interest. A low-profile, no-publicity approach is much more likely to enjoy the cooperation of credible black leaders and organizations.

'What have you to offer?': Many black South Africans suspect that American concern is inherently shallow and, therefore, they initially are likely to be less than enthusiastic. Building trust and acceptance takes time and persistence. Acceptance largely comes when the donor shows a commitment to learn about South Africa from the black perspective. There is a fine line between what some interviewees perceived as contrived empathy and a sincere commitment to the future of South Africa. The point is that if one has nothing to offer but sympathy, black South Africans are not likely to be enthusiastic.

Expect political flak: The complexity of South African politics makes it difficult not to draw criticism from one quarter or another. Americans need to understand the nuances of the political situation in South Africa and be conscious of the fact that every action has a political connotation. What is perceived positively by one group might be denounced by another.

Do your homework: For the reasons discussed above and because most black leaders have very demanding schedules, it is important that organizations and individuals without previous experience with South Africa do their homework before they go to South Africa.

Interviewees argued vigorously that critical views from blacks should not be taken to mean that all projects should be abandoned. On the contrary, it was argued that awareness of the issues affecting blacks' attitudes toward Americans would enhance the prospects for a mutually beneficial relationship. Despite the generally negative perceptions that most black leaders have of Americans, blacks are ready to allow those who approach the situation with sensitivity a chance to prove themselves. Moreover, as one interviewee put it, "South Africa is a society in turmoil. Much will be broken down, but that which blacks have adopted as their own will form the foundation of the new order."

I.
THE
POLITICAL COMPLEXITIES
OF SOUTH AFRICA

South Africa's history of racial oppression and black political resistance has created a complex political situation that affects almost every dimension of South African society. Many well intentioned initiatives have run aground on the complexities of South African politics, and although it is not possible to escape the political dimension, it is possible to gain acceptance among black South Africans through sensitivity to the political aspirations and social needs of blacks.

A BRIEF POLITICAL HISTORY

Although South Africa's political system is based on the pattern of racial segregation that was established when the country was first settled, it was not until 1948 that the newly elected National Party government began to legislate the radical ethnic and racial division of the country. The apartheid policy of the National Party government was premised upon Afrikaner nationalism that had gained momentum in the wake of the 1933 depression. Many Afrikaners were compelled to migrate to the cities in search of work, and there they came up against the predominance of English-speaking South Africans in business and industry, as well as the burgeoning urban black labor force. Afrikaner nationalism had as its aim the alleviation of poverty among Afrikaners, the political advancement of Afrikaners, and the rigorous separation of black and white.

Doctrinaire apartheid: The policy of apartheid or racial separation was aimed at the removal of all blacks from "white" South Africa and their confinement to ethnically defined homelands. Blacks were to be permitted in the white metropolitian areas only as temporary laborers. Moreover, legislation enforced racial segregation in all spheres, including a prohibition on inter-racial marriage and sex, as well as restrictions on black job mobility, and racially mixed social, residential and educational facilities.

In 1953 a system of "bantu education" designed to restrain the rate of black social and economic advancement was introduced in line with the government's policy that education should not awaken in blacks expectations of equality with whites.

Furthermore, blacks were barred from enrolling at the existing, predominantly white, universities, and separate universities for blacks were set up in the homelands.

The homelands: The homeland concept, the crux of the apartheid policy, sought to confine blacks to ethnically defined territories constituting only 13 percent of the South African land area. Blacks were denied all rights except the qualified right to sell their labor in the remaining "white" areas. Blacks' right to reside or seek work outside of the homelands was regulated by "influx control" laws that required blacks to carry an identification document establishing the legality of their presence in a "white" area.

Of the 10 homelands, four — Transkei, Ciskei, Venda and Bophuthatswana — are nominally independent (Appendix I). A fifth, KwaNdebele, was scheduled for "independence" in December 1986. However, after a period of bloody insurrection by residents of the region who opposed independence, these plans have been shelved. Blacks resident in the nominally independent homelands or of the same ethnic group as an independent homeland, even though they may not have been born in the area or ever lived there, were stripped of their South African citizenship and forced to take the citizenship of their designated homeland. The government's design was that eventually there would be no black South Africans.

The distinction between independent and non-independent homelands is essentially technical, since all remain politically and economically beholden to the central government. However, some homeland leaders, such as Enos Mabuza of Kangwane and KwaZulu's Gatsha Buthelezi, while functioning within the framework of the homeland system, have steadfastly refused independence. Although such leaders are often rhetorically bold in their challenges to government authority — Mabuza recently held discussions with the exiled liberation group the African National Congress (ANC) in Lusaka, and Buthelezi demands, among other things, the release of imprisoned ANC leader Nelson Mandela before he will be party to government negotiations — their detractors denounce them as collaborators with apartheid.

Buthelezi is a controversial figure. On the one hand, his support of a non-violent, pro-capitalist solution to the South African political impasse appeals to many white South Africans and to a significant international constituency. On the other hand, his persistent attempts to discredit the ANC, opposition to disinvestment and allegations of attacks on other anti-apartheid groups that oppose Inkatha have alienated the majority of black South Africans.

Reformed apartheid: Various factors, including international political pressure, black restiveness and the need to sustain economic growth, have compelled the government in recent years to make revisions to doctrinaire apartheid. As a result, during the 1970s restrictions on black job mobility were lifted and Africans were given the right to form trade unions. Furthermore, in 1984 the government added separate chambers for "colored" (mixed race) and Indian representatives to the previously all white parliament. Africans were excluded from the new "tri-cameral" government.

However, the government granted Africans the right to reside permanently in the segregated urban townships abutting the white metropolitian areas by permitting them, for the first time, to own property and introducing a system of elected black municipal administration in these areas. Moreover, the government has moved to scrap some apartheid legislation such as the prohibition on mixed marriages and the influx control laws.

The abolition of the harshest aspects of influx control — restricting black mobility and the right to reside permanently outside the homelands — does not signal the end of the homeland system. Recent revisions of the influx control laws have not restored South African citizenship to the nearly 4 million blacks resident in the four nominally independent homelands. Whereas government reforms stop short of dismantling the pillars of apartheid, there is evidence of a more open-ended approach to the issue of black political rights. The government has indicated that it is prepared to countenance black representation in the central government, but it remains vehemently opposed to any dispensation that might lead to a majority black government. Even so, the revision of traditional apartheid has led to divisions within the formerly monolithic facade of Afrikanerdom and has changed the face of white politics.

White politics: Afrikaners have traditionally supported the ruling National Party, but in 1982 more reactionary members of the party who oppose any departure from doctrinaire apartheid broke ranks to form the Conservative Party. Although the National Party has a virtually unassailable parliamentary majority, the Conservative Party enjoys significant support among working class and rural Afrikaners. Moreover, in an effort to obstruct government reforms, the Conservative Party seeks to build support among the predominantly Afrikaner police force and civil service.

Whites generally and Afrikaners in particular fear that they will be politically and culturally engulfed by the black majority. Thus, the National Party has been able to expand its traditional constituency to include a sizable proportion of the English-speaking community. Moreover, Afrikanerdom has evolved from its agrarian roots into a principally urbanized, middle class society having much in common with the traditionally middle class English. Working class and rural Afrikaners, on the other hand, find themselves largely estranged from mainstream Afrikanerdom. This group feels the most imperiled by the prospect of black advancement and thus exploits the ethnocentric emotions that gave Afrikaner nationalism momentum in the 1930s and '40s.

In contrast, historically the English-speaking community has been more liberally inclined toward black political advancement and social integration. This relative liberalism is based on the English community's historical domination of the economy that has traditionally imparted a sense of class security. Many argue that the economic interests of the English community benefited from apartheid's maintenance of a cheap and easily exploited black labor supply. Be that as it may, now that the economic interests of this group seem at risk from rising black activism, most English-speaking whites look to the National Party government to secure these interests and are no more racially accommodating than are mainstream Afrikaners.

Those English-speaking whites that do not support the National Party generally put their weight behind the Progressive Federal Party (PFP). This party is currently the official opposition in the white house of parliament, but it appears to face a serious challenge for this position from the Conservative Party. The PFP has traditionally propagated a non-racial vote within a federal structure, and since the repeal of legislation forbidding racially mixed political parties it has begun recruiting black members in an effort to establish non-racial credentials.

Black resistance: Organized black political resistance to white domination manifested itself long before 1948 and the advent of apartheid. On the eve of the institution of the Union of South Africa in 1910, blacks convened the South African Native Convention to protest the exclusion of Africans from the union government. Two years later the leaders of the Native Convention founded the African National Congress (ANC).

Although the ANC has been the foremost black political movement since then, numerous other groups — such as the South African Indian Congress (SAIC) and the white dominated South African Congress of Democrats — played an important role in mobilizing black resistance. In 1955 the principal activist organizations formed an alliance for the formulation of a set of common political aims that would become known as the Freedom Charter (Appendix II). Although different organizations subscribe to the Freedom Charter, the provisions of this document have become synonymous with the ideals of the ANC.

The Charter consists of a list of basic rights and freedoms. Beginning by reaffirming the multiracial character of South African society, it goes on to promise equal status for all "national groups"; to argue for the transfer of the mines, the banks and "monopoly industry" to the ownership of "the people as a whole"; to guarantee equal opportunities to all who wish "to trade or manufacture"; and to advocate the redivision of land "among those who work it," as well as free compulsory education and other welfare provisions with regard to health, housing, the aged and the disabled.

Although the Charter unites different groups, it has also been a divisive factor in black politics. In 1959, members of the ANC who rejected the Freedom Charter, on the grounds that it paid too much attention to securing white support and neglected the tenets of African nationalism, formed the Pan-Africanist Congress (PAC). Although one of the principal points of difference between the ANC and the PAC was the PAC's insistence that leadership of the black struggle be in black hands, there was also the feeling that the Freedom Charter offered only ideals and lacked any practical political strategy. Although the PAC's goals were no more clear than those of the ANC, in principle the PAC propagated a more radical socialist restructuring of society than the ANC supported at that time.

The PAC had a legal existence of slightly more than a year before it was driven underground and into exile along with the ANC following the shooting of 69 black protesters by police at Sharpeville in March 1960. Both organizations were declared illegal, and both subsequently produced insurgent wings to continue the struggle through underground tactics and sabotage.

After the banishment of the two nationalist movements, the focus of black resistance shifted beyond the country's borders. Blacks inside the country were quiescent until the early 1970s when a rash of strikes in the Durban area — to protest low wages and the escalating cost of living — marked a reawakening of internal black activism.

CONTEMPORARY BLACK POLITICS

The renewed resistance was attributable in large part to the increasing popularity of the philosophy of black consciousness during the late 1960s. The leading proponents of black consciousness argued that the key problem in mobilizing black resistance was psychological. Thus, after generations of oppression and paternalism, black consciousness exhorted blacks to draw on indigenous cultural traditions in asserting their individual human dignity. Black consciousness sought to cultivate in blacks a social identity independent of white liberal concepts of African integration into a Western capitalist society.

Put simply, black consciousness holds that blacks must be responsible for their own liberation and rejects white participation in the struggle. Adherents of this philosophy describe it as "an attitude of mind" fundamental to the psychological liberation of blacks after centuries of white suppression. Although the tenets of black consciousness are often perceived by whites as racist, adherents describe the philosophy as "pro-black," not "anti-white."

Although black consciousness was initially an intellectual movement with roots in the black university campuses, a number of organizations emerged with the aim of energizing a broader community. The most significant of these were the South African Students' Organization (SASO) — the first all black student organization — founded in 1969, and the Black People's Convention (BPC), established in 1972 by the leaders of SASO and other individuals drawn from several religious and educational bodies. SASO and the BPC played an important part in mobilizing the wave of black activism that manifested itself principally in student protests on black university campuses and industrial action by black workers in the early 1970s.

However, the watershed in the re-emergence of black activism was the 1976 Soweto uprising. The immediate consequence was a resurgence of black political consciousness and renewed organization that laid the foundation for the mass mobilization of blacks in the early 1980s.

In the last decade new internal political organizations have emerged to take the place of the nationalist movements in exile. Moreover, the exile movements have themselves drawn strength from the resurgence of activism. After the 1976 Soweto uprising an estimated 8,000 young blacks fled the country and were absorbed into the cadres of the African National Congress in exile.

The influx of young blood and the renewed restiveness in South Africa gave the ANC the opportunity to reassert itself as the predominant liberation organization. Moreover, many of the young activists were incarcerated after 1976 in the same prisons with ANC leaders such as Nelson Mandela and Walter Sisulu. After their release a significant number of these young leaders were firm converts to the values of non-racialism as espoused by the ANC and the Freedom Charter. The converts were persuaded that the tenets of black consciousness and non-racialism as espoused by the Freedom Charter are not mutually exclusive. They argue that black consciousness is a psychological affirmation of human dignity fundamental to an egalitarian society. This approach was by no means universal; a number of key disciples of the black consciousness movement were not influenced by incarceration to change their political beliefs. Thus the new generation of black political activists was divided between those that subscribe to the non-racial principles of the Freedom Charter and the ANC, and those that interpreted black conciousness as the basis of a more radical socialist restructuring of society.

The Azanian People's Organization: The organizational manifestations of the black consciousness movement were not very extensive, but its influence in cultivating the spirit of resistance among student groups was a significant factor in the nationwide insurrection that began in June 1976. What started as a protest by black students in Soweto against the use of Afrikaans as the medium of instruction in black schools — organized by a local affiliate of the black consciousness movement — became the spark for a major rebellion when police opened fire on the protesters, killing two.

In the security clampdown that followed more than a year of nationwide rioting, the black consciousness movement and all of its affiliates were banned. However, in 1978 supporters of black consciousness regrouped under the banner of the Azanian People's Organization (Azapo).

Although Azapo is careful to emphasize its organizational autonomy, in the arena of legally permissible political activity it is the most influential vehicle for the political tradition represented outside South Africa by the Pan-Africanist Congress. From its inception Azapo announced that it would direct its activities toward the involvement of the black working class and incorporated a class analysis into its policy.

Azapo's main aim is the establishment of a "non-racial and socialist workers' republic of Azania." Part of Azapo's socialist agenda is to combat American imperialism, and consequently the organization is vociferous in its denunciation of American foreign policy. Moreover, Azapo's anti-capitalist position makes it a strong proponent of the withdrawal of American business from South Africa.

In 1983, Azapo was responsible for convening a "National Forum," attended by a large number of political organizations, community groups and trade unions that rally to the banner of black consciousness. Although the initial purpose of the National Forum was to coordinate opposition to the institution of the tricameral parliament, it has subsequently taken on a life of its own as an informal affiliation of black consciousness and socialist oriented groups. Meetings of the National Forum are used to debate ideological and policy issues, and to provide intellectual guidance to the socialist persuasion in black politics.

Although Azapo is generally perceived as the contemporary organizational manifestation of the black consciousness movement, the influence of the black consciousness philosophy transcends any single organization. Supporters of the Freedom Charter and black consciousness advocates alike ascribe considerable importance to the influence of black consciousness in reinforcing black assertiveness in the face of persistent repression. As one interviewee put it, "Because people are trapped in a dehumanizing system, there is constant need to reaffirm their humanity."

The United Democratic Front: The conversion of the bulk of the 1976 political leadership to non-racialism led to a popular resurgence of that concept and support for the principles of the Freedom Charter. Many community groups and student and political organizations formed in the early 1980s, such as the Release Mandela Campaign and the Congress of South African Students, subscribed to the tenets of non-racialism and called for full political equality. Moreover, a significant body of the emergent black labor movement adopted a similar position.

Spurred by common opposition to the exclusion of Africans from the tricameral parliament, some 600 community based and workers' organizations sharing a common loyalty to the ANC and the Freedom Charter formed the United Democratic Front in mid-1983. This loosely structured association rapidly became a populist movement claiming more than 1 million members — the largest anti-apartheid group in the country.

Reflecting the non-racial, egalitarian principles of the African National Congress, the UDF includes a small number of white organizations in its ranks, such as the End Conscription Campaign (ECC). Leaders of the UDF believe the organization has an important role to play in advancing non-racial cooperation and fostering a broad based alliance of anti-apartheid groups.

The concept of non-racialism is variously described by supporters of the UDF interviewed by IRRC as "color blindness" and "a laissez faire attitude toward race," but most make it clear that blacks are tired of being dominated by whites and, therefore, are opposed to a predominance of whites in leadership positions. They argue that until blacks have sufficient confidence in "cooperative non-racialism," blacks will be reserved in their "embrace of whites."

The UDF is a loosely structured umbrella assocation of autonomous organizations, and its principal significance, therefore, is in mobilizing united political resistance. The loosely structured nature of the organization makes it a more difficult target for state repression, since it would be virtually impossible to outlaw all of the UDF's constituent organizations. However, the disadvantage is that the UDF has no cohesive policy and difficulty in coordinating the activities of affiliate groups. Support for the UDF is based mostly on the organization's reputation as a populist front for the ANC.

In October 1986, the South African government declared the UDF an "affected" organization in terms of South African fundraising laws, thus prohibiting the organization from receiving funds from sources outside of South Africa. This action is not expected to immobilize the organization, since the prohibition does not apply to affiliates of the UDF, and leaders of the UDF are confident that alternative funding channels will be developed.

The African National Congress: After the ANC was outlawed in 1960, the organization initiated an insurgency campaign directed from neighboring southern African countries. The aim of the campaign has been to undermine the morale of the white minority government through sporadic sabotage and guerrilla attacks on government installations. At the same time, the ANC has successfully cultivated international recognition as the principal black South African liberation movement.

Recently the ANC has escalated the insurgency campaign to include non-government targets in response to attacks by the South African security forces on ANC bases. It has also recently engaged in highly publicized discussions with white South African business, student and church leaders, as well as leaders of the Progressive Federal Party. However, the ANC's official position is that it will negotiate only about the unconditional transfer of political power, and there has been no recorded contact with South African government officials.

Some detractors of the ANC describe it as an "amorphous political movement" without a clear political focus. Although the Freedom Charter is described as a set of broad ideals that will direct public policy, more practically the ANC leaders speak of a form of social democracy akin to the Swedish model of socialism. However, the general wisdom is that the socialist ideals of a future ANC government would inevitably be tempered by political and economic realities.

The ANC has long campaigned for the withdrawal of international investors and the imposition of economic sanctions against South Africa as a means of weakening the apartheid regime. Moreover, the ANC argues for the redistribution of wealth in South Africa and the nationalization of key industries. The withdrawal of foreign companies from South Africa would lessen the hold that foreign investors have over the economy so as to facilitate the socialist restructuring of the economy after the advent of majority government.

ANC leader Nelson Mandela, imprisoned in 1962 for leaving the country without a passport and sentenced to life imprisonment in 1964 on charges of treason, has assumed mystical symbolism in the resistance struggle as the only leader who could successfully unite South African blacks. The government has recently made several proposals for Mandela's conditional release. The principal precondition is that Mandela renounce violence as a strategy of resistance and that the ANC abandon its insurgency campaign. Mandela in turn has set the state's cessation of violence against black resistance and the legalization of the ANC as conditions for an ANC ceasefire. Leaders of the ANC argue that the organization was forced to adopt a strategy of violence in response to the government's brutal repression of black resistance, after nearly 50 years of non-violent political protest.

Opinion polls have consistently shown the ANC to enjoy the support of the bulk of the black population. This fact together with the international standing of the ANC as the principal liberation movement has led various white South African business leaders, student groups and academics to engage in discussions with ANC leadership. Although these discussions have generally been described as "exploratory," they have certainly added to the prestige of the ANC both locally and internationally, and have underscored the expectation that the ANC will dominate a future majority government in South Africa.

The South African Communist Party: Formed in 1921, the South African Communist Party (SACP) initially focused on the lot of white workers, but later aligned itself with the black struggle against apartheid. In 1950, the SACP was declared an unlawful organization under the Suppression of Communism Act legislated by the South African parliament that year. The SACP went underground, and a number of its leaders joined the ranks of the ANC.

Although the SACP in exile maintains an independent identity, a number of the current ANC leaders are also members of the SACP. The influence of communists in the ANC is presented as one of the reasons why the government will not negotiate with the ANC. Leaders of the ANC deny that the communists have a controlling influence over the organization. Officials of the ANC interviewed by IRRC were dismissive of the charges that the ANC is a communist front. Other interviewees were derisive of the SACP as a party without a significant black following trying to benefit from the ANC's popularity. As one interviewee put it, "The SACP is not part of the indigenous black political structure and is simply riding on the coattails of the ANC" in order to attract popular support. Another interviewee pointed out that the SACP "is a movement founded by white intellectuals" and that blacks suspect that the SACP "has hegemonic designs that will never be tolerated by black people."

Nonetheless, there is evidence that the SACP is becoming more assertive in an effort to distinguish itself as an autonomous part of the liberation movement. One aspect of this new role has been the unfurling of the communist flag alongside the colors of the ANC at political funerals. In addition, a number of interviewees spoke of organized groups of SACP supporters that have emerged as distinct elements within established black political organizations. However, most interviewees ascribed the more public support for the SACP in large measure to ideological naivete on the part of many young blacks and to political bravado. One interviewee explained that support for communism is seen by many younger blacks as the most extreme rejection of the status quo, but it does not necessarily signal a significant ideological trend in black politics.

The Pan-Africanist Congress: Although the PAC does not enjoy the same popular support among black South Africans as the ANC, it is far from moribund. Indeed, it was recently reported that PAC guerrillas had undergone training in Libya. Nonetheless, the PAC in exile has not maintained a high profile either on the international diplomatic front or in the domestic insurgency campaign. The reasons for this are a lack of effective leadership and the fact that "African nationalism" is an abstract concept that has failed to attract much support outside South Africa.

Supporters of the PAC are rankled by the fact that they are seldom included in discussions about the liberation struggle or the political future of South Africa. They believe the Western powers cultivate the ANC because its ideals most closely coincide with the West's own "imperialistic designs." Nonetheless, black consciousness adherents believe that the PAC will come into its own as a political force after the advent of majority government. As one PAC official put it, "The ANC might be the people's [liberation] movement, but it is not the people's party."

The black trade union movement: An important factor in the new era of black political mobilization was the legal recognition of black trade unions in 1979. The emergent black union movement is a democratic anomaly in a society that denies blacks any other representation. Inevitably the black unions took on a political role. Although only about 12 percent of the African work force (fewer than 1 million workers) is unionized, the union movement has a political influence far beyond its formal membership. As one union leader put it, "We are blacks before we are workers," and in the absence of other channels workers expect the unions to take up community issues and grievances.

At the end of 1985, 36 trade unions — representing some 500,000 workers — united under a single federation, the Congress of South African Trade Unions (Cosatu). The significance of Cosatu is primarily political; it has assumed an overtly political posture and has claimed a series of political objectives in pursuit of which it intends to organize its members.

However, the division between black consciousness and non-racialism is also reflected in the union movement. Cosatu member unions are generally identified with the non-racial position, while those unions that subscribe to the principles of black consciousness are grouped in two smaller federations — the Council of Unions of South Africa (Cusa) and the Azanian Congress of Trade Unions (Azactu). These two federations have announced plans to merge their membership under the banner of a new organization to be known as the National Council of Trade Unions (NCTU).

Unionization has provided a platform for democratic organization and developing political awareness that has had an important spillover effect in the organization of many community political associations.

Inkatha: Of the homeland leaders only Chief Gatsha Buthelezi cultivates a national following. The Inkatha movement led by Buthelezi has significant support among older members of the Zulu ethnic group — political analysts at the University of Natal estimate support for Buthelezi among Zulus at between 40 and 60 percent. However, Inkatha is increasingly challenged by younger Zulus in the urban areas of Natal, and sporadic conflicts between supporters of the UDF and Inkatha have occurred. An Inkatha supporter of longstanding interviewed by IRRC admitted that many young Zulus are dissaffected with what he called "tribal politics," but he suggested many were caught up in an "emotional tide of populist support for the UDF and the ANC" and that most youngsters are ideologically unsophisticated and "politically fickle."

Polls indicate that, outside of Natal, Inkatha has only marginal support among blacks, but Buthelezi's pro-capitalist stance has ensured the support of the white business community, and he is often described as the trump in a black-white moderate political coalition that will shut out the ANC. Moreover, Buthelezi has from time to time formed alliances with other political groups, such as the colored Labor Party and the white Progressive Federal Party, in an effort to broaden his political base.

Although ostensibly a cultural movement, Inkatha is organized along pseudo-military lines, making it a most effective mobilizing machine, but also intolerant of dissidents. Consequently, Inkatha has gained a reputation for dealing ruthlessly with its opponents. Moreover, Inkatha members are suspected of responsibility for sporadic assaults on supporters of anti-apartheid groups and a number of political assassinations in the Natal area in recent years. Furthermore, in May 1986 Inkatha spawned a new labor federation — the United Workers' Union of South Africa — to offset the influence of more radical labor unions and to create an anti-disinvestment platform in the black labor movement.

Buthelezi is the only black political leader of any international standing opposed to American business withdrawal from South Africa. This is a major point of conflict between Buthelezi and other black leaders, particularly the ANC. Although Buthelezi was a young member of the ANC and once enjoyed filial relations with ANC leaders, he is now accused of being a "sellout," and Nelson Mandela recently refused Buthelezi's request for a meeting.

BLACK DIVISIVENESS

The cooptation of blacks in the implementation and administration of apartheid is the most broadly divisive factor in black politics. Blacks who participate in the institutions of apartheid, such as homeland governments and black municipal authorities, as well as blacks who work for apartheid enforcement agencies, such as the security forces, are targets of black resentment and violent reprisal. In order to quell popular opposition, some homeland governments — Venda, Transkei and Ciskei — are brutally repressive and are as much a target of black political resistance as the white regime.

On a different level there is conflict among blacks over scarce and inadequate community resources. Blacks possessing the legal right to reside and work in the "white" metropolitan centers are at an economic, social and political advantage over those blacks constrained by the remnants of the influx control system to live in the homelands. This division between "urban insiders" and "rural outsiders" has come to constitute an added dimension to the ethnic "divide and rule" basis of apartheid, whereby the government has traditionally exploited black ethnic divisions for its own political purposes.

The increasing urban migration of rural blacks further overburdens black urban facilities. Moreover, there is competition for jobs as unemployment among blacks exceeds 30 percent. The result is tension between settled blacks and newcomers. This tension from time to time translates into physical violence between the two groups. Most recently black settlements outside of Durban were the scene of protracted battles between settled groups and newcomers in the opening months of 1986.

These tensions are intertwined with political conflicts, and a recent phenomenon has been the emergence of vigilante groups within many established black townships and squatter communities. The vigilantes are older members of the community who have grouped together to maintain order in the face of increasing lawlessness by younger black groups. These black groups have acquired the name of "comrades," reflecting their assumed status as the vanguard of the black liberation struggle. The "comrades" have taken it upon themselves to eradicate blacks who are perceived to be less than committed to the "struggle." Although the vigilantes have generally been described as defenders of the status quo, some observers believe that the fight is more about territorial control and the traditional authority of elders of the community than about political inclinations. However, government security forces are suspected of assisting the more conservative older factions, thus marking vigilantes as "collaborators" in the eyes of the comrades. Large sections of the Crossroads squatter camp near Cape Town were razed in two weeks of fighting between vigilante groups and comrades in May 1986.

Many black community leaders interviewed by IRRC described evidence of government security forces supplying arms to different factions in the black community to exacerbate the internecine tension. The security forces are accused of using black-on-black violence as an excuse to crack down on political dissidents.

Within the broader arena of black resistance the principal ideological division is between the "Charterists" — those subscribing to the Freedom Charter and affiliated with the UDF and by implication the ANC — and the supporters of black consciousness and a more radical socialist inclination affiliated with Azapo and the PAC. Although this division has ideological roots, it has been exacerbated in recent times by the unreal expectation that black government is imminent. This has given rise to a struggle for political influence and power.

Because the black consciousness camp fears that an ANC government will not tolerate political opposition, they believe they must establish their claim to a share in political power now, or fight for it after the advent of majority government. Leading supporters of black consciousness say that many blacks are waiting to see what sort of liberation the ANC will deliver, implying that if a future government dominated by the ANC were perceived to be too moderate, blacks would continue to advance more extreme positions. Black consciousness advocates speak openly of the prospect of a "second struggle" after the advent of black majority government for the establishment of a socialist state. The Charterists, on the other hand, benefit from the populist support enjoyed by the ANC as the principal liberation movement.

These differences first developed into violent confrontation during the visit of Sen. Edward Kennedy to South Africa at the invitation of the UDF in January 1985. Azapo supporters opposed to the visit clashed openly with members of the UDF. Since then the bitter rivalry between Azapo and the UDF has resulted in sporadic assaults and killings by supporters of each group against the other.

Leaders of both the UDF and Azapo interviewed by IRRC acknowledged that their supporters were involved in physical reprisals against one another, but also admitted that emotions are running so high that supporters are often beyond the control of leaders. Moreover, leaders of both camps said that black collaborators were armed and paid by government security forces to exploit the factionalism by staging attacks on leading supporters of one side or the other. Saths Cooper, president of Azapo, said that we "set out to make the country ungovernable for the government, but we have made it ungovernable for everyone." He explained that the ideological differences have been "marked in blood" and as a result "there is a legacy of revenge" that puts reason beyond the pale of the average supporter.

STRATEGIES OF RESISTANCE

Two developments provided the spark for the current wave of black unrest. One was the establishment of the tricameral parliament and the second was the worsening economy, which made it more difficult for Africans to meet rising costs of living and caused them to resent especially rent increases in their segregated townships. In September 1984, after a year of protest and class boycotts by school students, rioting broke out in African townships south of Johannesburg.

The government reacted by sending army troops into the riot areas to restore order. Hundreds of activist leaders were rounded up and imprisoned. Unlike 1976, black protesters resisted this time, mostly with stones and homemade petrol bombs, but later with firearms and grenades as well. In the first two weeks 35 blacks were killed. The ANC, which had been caught off guard by the 1976 uprising, was quick to respond to the new uprising and called on blacks to make the country "ungovernable." The uprising turned into a national rebellion that has been sustained for more than two years and has left more than 2,000 blacks dead.

Several factors have combined to enable black resistance to withstand the most brutal repression in the country's history. Of particular importance have been the growth of the black labor movement and the emergence of alliances between community groups and labor unions. The first mass demonstration of worker-community solidarity occurred during November 1984 when between 300,000 and 800,000 workers in the Witwatersrand area stayed away from work for two days. The "stayaway" was held in support of demands by African pupils for democratically elected student representative councils, the withdrawal of security forces from the townships, the release of all political detainees and the abandonment of rent, service and bus fare increases. The November stayaway was supported by 37 union, student and community organizations, some of which had a national following. Shorter, regionally based stayaways have been organized regularly in various parts of the country since then to coincide with school boycotts and political funerals or to protest state repression.

The most significant manifestation of the mobilization of community based and worker organizations was the formation of the UDF. The initial focus of UDF activity was to protest the tricameral parliament and to mobilize resistance to the system of municipal administration that the government had imposed in African townships after the 1976 riots. Urban Africans, rejecting this system, demonstrated their disapproval by largely boycotting elections for African town councillors. Activists demanded that town councillors resign and after August 1984, violent reprisal, ranging from firebombing to assassination, was increasingly taken against those who resisted. By the end of 1985 only three of the 104 African town councils were still functioning.

Furthermore, community organizations began to organize black consumer boycotts of white businesses, initially to pressure local whites into improving the infrastructure of black townships and providing community facilities. The first consumer boycott was spearheaded by the residents' association of Cradock, a small town in the Eastern Cape. Gladwell Makhawula, president of the association, explained in a recent press interview that no whites ever came to the black township so "we decided to boycott their shops to try and make them come and see the real conditions under which we live." Later boycott leaders stepped up their demands, calling on local white businessmen to pressure the government for fundamental political change. The consumer boycotts, particularly in the smaller towns of the Eastern Cape, were successful in many cases in motivating whites to improve conditions in the local townships and to meet with government leaders to present black political demands.

The effectiveness of consumer boycotts and work stoppages reflects the growing solidarity between older and younger blacks. In 1976, parents were oblivious to the growing resentment among their children. Ten years later the demands of students are echoed by their parents.

An outstanding example of the new unity between students and parents is the formation of the National Education Crisis Committee (NECC) at the end of 1985. After nearly two years of school boycotts by students, a conference of students, teachers and parents was convened to consider the implications of a call by students to boycott classes again in 1986. The conference resolved that the students should return to school at least until March while it demanded of the government that it withdraw its troops from the townships, release political prisoners, unban the Congress of South African Students, rebuild schools damaged in the two years of student protest, and provide free tuition and books for students of all race groups.

By the end of March, as more than 1,500 representatives of students, teachers and parents met in Durban, few of the demands had been met. Rather than sanctioning another school boycott, the conference resolved that parents, teachers and students must collectively take over schools and devise new teaching techniques and curricula based on "people's education." The conference appointed a commission to revise the school curriculum and to make specific recommendations on the course content of "people's education."

One of the lessons that black political leaders have learned from Soweto 1976 is that to be effective, black political organizations must be able to avoid being banned altogether and to survive the detention of their leaders. The UDF and the organizations that rally to its banner tend to have a decentralized leadership. Moreover, the UDF is not a single organization, but a coalition of more than 600 community, student and union groups. Thus it is more difficult for the state to cripple the organization by simply imprisoning a small group of leaders as it did in 1976. Moreover, while it is possible for the government to outlaw the UDF, it would be virtually impossible to eradicate its influence as a populist movement that has spawned scores of informally constituted community groups and in whose name black communities across the country have been politically mobilized.

However, the looseness of the leadership structure of the UDF and many community groups has made them, by definition, less democratic organizations, creating other problems. The black unions are formally organized to ensure that leaders report back to the rank and file before they take major policy decisions; the community groups are not. The lack of accountabilty in many community groups and the UDF means that in many cases the leaders are out of touch with their grassroots, who in turn do not feel obligated to respect policy pronouncements by the leaders. As a result many of the more mature, seasoned leaders can no longer control younger, more zealous activists.

In many black townships, activists have formed "block committees" or "street committees" as a form of local government and "people's tribunals." Through these organizations activists have targeted perceived collaborators with the white authorities, such as black policemen, suspected police informers and those who are perceived to be less than committed in their observance of the community cause. Young activists have been responsible for a large number of gruesome atrocities against other blacks. As a result, many blacks are more fearful of retribution from community activists than of confrontation with the security forces. These "street committees" have been particularly effective in enforcing a sustained rent boycott by residents in Soweto and other black townships abutting Johannesburg.

BLACKS AND CAPITALISM

The charge that capitalism is the pivot of political and economic inequality has steadily gained currency in black politics. Adherents of the Freedom Charter emphasize capitalism as opposed to racism as the primary cause of exploitation and oppression. The black consciousness argument, on the other hand, perceives race and racial subjugation as the driving force. This view is encapsulated in the maxim, "in South Africa race determines class." Stripped to crude essentials, this means that workers are black and the owners of capital are white.

The term "racial capitalism" has been secured in the South African political vocabulary by its inclusion in the Manifesto of the People of Azania (Appendix III). The Manifesto, drawn up in June 1983 at the founding conference of the National Forum attended by more than 800 delegates representative of some 200 organizations, specifies racial capitalism as the "real enemy" and calls for the establishment of a non-racial socialist republic where the interests of the workers shall be paramount through worker control of the means of production, distribution and exchange.

Ignoring the technicalities of the interpretation of cause and effect, the most significant point of convergence between the two principal groupings in black politics is that the national liberation struggle is not merely against apartheid and race discrimination, but also against capitalism as the perceived primary cause of black oppression. Moreover, both groups share a similar vision of a socialist restructuring of the economy and society after "liberation."

The notion that capitalism is the flip side of the apartheid coin underscores black pressure for the withdrawal of foreign companies from South Africa. The argument is that foreign investment reinforces the government's ability to resist international and domestic pressure to end apartheid. The withdrawal of foreign companies was conceived as an element in the black resistance strategy aimed at accelerating the demise of the Pretoria regime. All the major black political groupings and the black labor unions, except Chief Buthelezi's Inkatha movement, support withdrawal. However, four opinion surveys conducted between January 1985 and June 1986 indicate that only a core of about 25 percent of black workers surveyed support withdrawal unconditionally.

BLACK POLITICS AND COMMUNITY DEVELOPMENT

Most community development initiatives are aimed at redressing the social, economic and political disadvantages of black South Africans. However, the underlying cause of black disadvantage is fundamentally political — in that political decisions by white South Africans have blocked black access to resources and opportunities — and blacks thus judge community development initiatives almost exclusively by their political relevance. Community development in South Africa is not aimed only at providing a base for community subsistence, but at empowering black South Africans to resist repression and build institutions that will form the groundwork of a new socio-political order. Consequently, most community development organizations have political affiliations. As one interviewee put it, "It is not possible to avoid the political flak, but if you choose your strategy carefully, people will judge you by your actions and not by their political prejudice."

There are various pointers to navigating through this political minefield, but all are founded upon a single premise — credibility with black South Africans.

THE CONSULTATION PROCESS

The credibility of any community development initiative in the eyes of the bulk of black South Africans depends on the approval of leading black activist groups. This political endorsement is in turn dependent upon the extent to which blacks perceive the initiative to reflect black political aspirations and social needs. The key to the legitimation and acceptability of any undertaking is an extensive process of consultation with recognized black leaders, as well as respected black political and community organizations.

This process can often be time consuming and cumbersome, but it is indispensable to the effectiveness and acceptability of any community development initiative. Blacks are generally cynical about "do goodism" and will not accept the bona fides of an initiative at face value. It is essential to build mutual trust between the donor and recipient. In the words of a prominent community leader, "proposals need to be internalized by black organizations; they need to be able to discuss (the proposal) with the broader community, to make their own input and to mold initiatives to their own requirements." He explained "that this imparts a sense of ownership and involvement" that would otherwise be lacking.

The consultation process is not to ratify a preconceived agenda, but more to mold a particular concept to meet the articulated requirements of black South Africans. To be effective, the consultation process requires a dispassionate ear, but also an astute understanding of the nuances of black politics and South African society. Since the object of the exercise is to lay a firm political foundation, it is particularly important that there be evenhanded consultation with non-racial and black consciousness groups. The prospects are that initial conceptions of the project will turn out very differently, but its chances of success will be much greater if it genuinely reflects black needs and elicits the cooperation of respected black leaders and organizations.

The consultation process should be conducted at three levels, and although there is a great deal of overlap between individuals and organizations at all three levels, consultation at one level will not substitute for consultation at the other levels.

Public black leadership: Although the sanction of internationally recognized black activist leaders, such as Nobel laureate Archbishop Desmond Tutu, the Rev. Allan Boesak and Winnie Mandela, is important in building credibility and may be useful in gaining access to the network of less public black leadership and community groups, interviewees agreed that far broader consultation is essential. One interviewee explained that "credibility cannot be bought, we are not impressed by big names." Another interviewee said that while the opinion of such leaders obviously has weight in the black community, "people on the edge of survival have a very different sense of priority."

On the practical level, it is unrealistic to expect leaders of this stature to sanction personally all community development initiatives or to meet every American exploratory mission to South Africa. Thus the prime focus of the consultation process is necessarily at the second and third level, but it is politic to keep first level leaders informed of developments and to seek their advice on a regular basis.

The organizational level: There is a network of organizations through which the legitimacy of any intiative may be ratified. This network includes the major union federations — Cosatu, Cusa and Azactu; the church — the South African Council of Churches and the Southern African Catholic Bishops' Conference; and the two principal internal resistance movements — the UDF and Azapo. These organizations have a national following and their cooperation is invaluable.

Grassroots: Although the first two levels of consultation provide an umbrella legitimacy and are essential in the trust building exercise, the ultimate test of acceptability is the participation of community based organizations. It is these organizations that are mostly responsible for the implementation of community development programs and most closely reflect the needs and aspirations of particular communities. The black civic associations that exist in almost every black township are an amalgam of smaller community groups — including youth, women's and church groups, as well as local unions and political organizations — and thus they reflect "grassroots" attitudes and are well placed to conduct consultations within local communities.

The role of the external resistance movements in the consultation process is also important. As one interviewee put it, "Blacks perceive the internal and external struggle as a continuum" and consultation with the ANC and PAC is, therefore, politically important. However, consultations with the external movements will not automatically lead to credibility with internal organizations. Leaders of both the ANC and the PAC take the position that there is no substitute for consultation with "the people" and internal organizations.

The question of what constitutes a "credible" community development organization is a matter of political perception. Some organizations are more politically acceptable than others to blacks. As discussed above, black society is generally divided into two groups, those that are referred to as "collaborators" — namely, blacks who are viewed as part of the apartheid structure — and "activists" — those who actively oppose apartheid and seek a radical transformation of society. The collaborators, an increasingly isolated minority, include members of the homeland governments and black town councils. Cooperation with any of these institutions will automatically exclude support from other blacks. There is particular sensitivity among activist blacks to any association with Inkatha.

In addition there are schisms between organizations that profess activist objectives.

PROGRESSIVE VERSUS STATUS QUO

Put simply, the principal difference in the activist community is between organizations that are perceived to be status quo oriented — even though their objectives might seem quite radical — and those that are perceived to be "progressive." Organizations that are committed to political change in South Africa, but singled out by interviewees as examples of organizations that are not perceived by blacks to be "progressive," include the Urban Foundation and the South African Institute of Race Relations. Interviewees argued that such organizations operate from an essentially white political perception, and therefore their motives will always be suspect. Interviewees explained that it is not simply a matter of black versus white leadership, but more a matter of the extent to which an organization reflects real black aspirations, as well as the political credentials of blacks involved.

Progressive organizations are perceived to be contributing to the black struggle for the restructuring of South African society. Whether they have explicitly political objectives or are non-political, they are judged largely by the extent to which blacks empathize with their objectives. Examples of progressive organizations identified by interviewees are the Legal Resources Center — a white-run organization — and the South African Committee for Higher Education (Sached) — a black-run organization — among many others. An interviewee explained that progressive organizations are "institutionalized in the black community" and enjoy the public support of recognized black leaders.

Among progressive organizations there are cleavages between those that follow a non-racial line and those that adhere to black consciousness principles. The latter organizations are not averse to working with selected non-racial or white "progressive" institutions, but they hold that leadership and decisionmaking power must remain in black hands. As discussed above, the difference between these two groups has translated into bitter rivalry within the black community. Often initiatives by one group or the other become the focus of such rivalry.

Although it is possible to avoid this factionalism through careful planning and evenhanded consultation, it is not possible to escape the broader black political struggle. This implies that a political choice has to be made. As one interviewee put it, "As far as blacks are concerned there are really only two options — either you are on the side of the black struggle or you are not — there are no half measures."

MAKING A POLITICAL CHOICE

Blacks are highly critical of initiatives that are aimed at "polishing the chains of apartheid" as Archbishop Tutu has put it. They believe initiatives must go beyond ameliorating the injustices of apartheid to lay the foundation for a new order by developing appropriate institutions and providing blacks with the necessary skills. In the words of one interviewee, "Blacks do not simply want to feel better about apartheid, we want to effect a fundamental redistribution of political power." A black community leader explained that "blacks will only respect those institutions that are a legitimate part of the black struggle," and everything else is suspect.

The implication is that association with "progressive" as opposed to "status quo" organizations, consultation with recognized activist leaders instead of collaborators, and the acceptance of "black terms" as against the imposition of preconceived plans reflects a choice for black political liberation. Undertakings that profess to be meeting the needs of blacks, but are not rooted in the black political struggle, will be dismissed as "papering over the cracks of apartheid." Politically suspect initiatives are likely to be rejected at the outset. Once political aspersions have been cast on a particular undertaking it is virtually impossible to redeem political credibility.

II.

PRIORITY AREAS FOR COMMUNITY DEVELOPMENT IN SOUTH AFRICA

Interviewees stressed that priorities for community development are interrelated and thus one is not necessarily more important than the other. However, there is agreement that the priorities fall broadly into three areas — alleviating black poverty, assisting the victims of apartheid and preparing the ground for majority government.

Although some interviewees responded with optimism about the prospects for a short term political transition, a number confided their despondency at the escalating violence in the country and the increasing disregard for human life and civil liberties. All agreed that it is not possible to predict with any confidence how long the political turmoil will continue. They also agreed that political equality will not signal immediate social and economic equality for all South Africans. As one interviewee put it, "The need for an affirmative focus in social services will not disappear with the advent of majority government in South Africa — the disadvantaged will remain socially and economically disadvantaged for some considerable time."

Those interviewed agreed that there are number of basic assumptions that influence perceptions of the priorities for community development:

— the number of black South Africans living below the poverty line will continue to increase as unemployment continues to grow, and the prospects of generating sufficient employment opportunities through the conventional benefits of economic growth are remote;

— although there is no real food shortage in South Africa now, by the year 2000, at the current rate of increase in agricultural production and at the current population growth rate, the country will not be able to feed itself;

— the majority of Africans will continue to live in the rural areas, and even if significant land redistribution were to take place, the rural areas would remain disadvantaged in terms of basic infrastructure and community services;

- the population growth rate among Africans will not decline until there is a real improvement in the standard of living among Africans, and the growth rate is likely to remain highest among the rural population where subsistence is the most difficult;

- the educational inequalities for Africans will not be bridged in the short term;

- an egalitarian government would find it difficult to muster the resources to meet the demands for black housing and basic community facilities;

- a radical change in the political system will not necessarily lead to a rapid correction in social and economic disparities, and might initially lead to a worsening of conditions.

Although the problems of black impoverishment and underdevelopment are obviously a function of the present political system, a future majority government will be hard pressed to meet the social and economic expectations of black South Africans. But, many blacks have been led to believe that if apartheid were removed there would be an immediate change in their quality of life. Many black political leaders realize that this is far from reality and express concern that the inability of a future government to deliver a short-term improvement in the lot of the average black will lead to further political instability and dissent.

Many of those interviewed stressed that a more sophisticated understanding of the factors influencing economic development is essential not only for alleviating black poverty, but also for enhancing the stability of a future majority government. They argued that black social and economic disadvantage would not be eliminated by the fact of political equality and that community development should therefore focus on the root causes of what some described as a "poverty-dependency cycle."

THE POVERTY–DEPENDENCY CYCLE

The principal factors shaping the pattern of economic development in South Africa are population growth and migration, access to scarce resources (particularly water), the state of the rural economy (particularly subsistence food production and land distribution), economic growth and employment creation.

All these factors are interdependent — South Africa's population is growing at a rate faster than that at which the economy can provide employment; at the same time, natural population growth in, as well as the relocation of black people to, the homelands has led to chronic overcrowding in these areas. Overcrowding in turn has impoverished agricultural land, leading to the collapse of the subsistence rural economy. As a result, rural Africans increasingly depend upon the industrial/urban sector for subsistence. The implications are large scale unemployment, rural poverty and increasing urban migration, as well as increasing social and political tensions arising from the economy's incapacity to cope with the social and political demands made upon it. Indeed, a recent South African government report suggested that unless South Africa acted on these issues now, it faces large scale social unrest where political rights will be forgotten in the battle for food and water. There is evidence that this battle has already begun.

Inadequate infrastructure: A principal factor in black impoverishment is the inadequacy of basic community facilities and services such as housing, water supply, sanitation and waste disposal. The standard of these facilities varies dramatically from the larger urban townships — a number of which have been electrified in recent years and which have water borne sewer systems — to the smaller urban black settlements — most of which do not have electricity, drainage or piped sewerage — and the rural villages and resettlement sites where running water is rare, or in scarce supply, and other facilities are non-existent.

There is an estimated backlog of 500,000 homes needed for Africans already settled in black townships adjacent to the white urban centers. The result is acute overcrowding of existing accommodation — the average four room home in Soweto outside Johannesburg houses 13 people — and an increase in shanty settlements on the periphery of established black townships.

Overcrowding and impoverishment of rural areas: Approximately 55 percent of the African population, about 13 million people, live on the 13 percent of the South African land area that makes up the ethnic homelands. Of these people, about 3 million have been forcibly removed from their traditional settlements in "white" South Africa and resettled in the homelands. The total population of the homelands increased from 4 million in 1960 to more than 13 million in 1986.

The principal means of subsistence in the homelands is agriculture. The overpopulation of the land has led to the impoverishment of the soil and the collapse of the subsistence rural economy. This situation has been exacerbated by prolonged severe drought over large parts of the country, as well as the scarcity of irrigation facilities and other agricultural factors.

One of the most serious consequences of the overcrowding of the homelands has been the almost complete deforestation of these regions resulting in severe erosion of the soil and ecological damage, but also depriving most rural homes of any affordable source of energy for cooking and heating.

Urban migration: By 1980 an estimated 40 percent of the African population was urbanized. This figure is expected to grow to around 53 percent, approximately 17.3 million, by the year 2000. The collapse of the subsistence agriculture sector in the homelands has greatly increased the migration of Africans to the "white" metropolitan regions in search of employment. The increasing numbers of urban migrants further overburden the rudimentary facilities in established black townships.

Unemployment: Since the mid-1960s the industrialized sector of the South African economy has been increasingly unable to absorb the expanding work force. About 30 percent of the economically active African population (approximately 4 million) is unemployed — with no source of income — or "underemployed" — employed in low productivity, low income jobs. Unemployment has increased rapidly over the last five years because of the sustained recession in the South African economy. Academics in the Eastern Cape, where the motor industry is the chief employer, estimate that unemployment among Africans in that area is as high as 80 percent.

An estimated average annual growth rate of 5.5 percent is needed to contain structural unemployment at around 6 percent. By contrast the average annual growth rate during the boom years of the 1970s was only 3.6 percent, and it dropped to 0.1 percent for the first five years of the 1980s. Government planners confirm that the country has a permanent structural unemployment problem, and unemployment among Africans is expected to top 40 percent by 1990. Judging by the disruption of the economy over the last two years, this percentage could be considerably higher.

Population growth: The African population is increasing by an estimated 3 percent per year. At this rate of increase it is estimated that South Africa will have insufficient water resources and food producing capacity to support its population by the year 2000. Birth control is a politically and culturally sensitive issue for most Africans, who view it as a stratagem to perpetuate white political hegemony. It probably will not be possible to reduce the African birth rate until there is an improvement in the standard of living.

Inferior black education: Education has been manipulated through the institution in the early 1950s of "bantu" education, designed to restrain the rate of black social and economic advancement.

The result is that despite significant increases in government expenditure on black education — from $70 million in 1980 to $450 million in 1986 — blacks are grossly undereducated in relation to whites. The median period of schooling in 1980 was 9.2 years for whites, but only two years for Africans. The functional illiteracy rate among Africans is near 50 percent, and fewer than 30 percent of university students are blacks. The slow pace of black social and economic advancement and the inferior standards of black education have gradually undermined blacks' perception of the value of education. One of the consequences is the percentage of black students entering the 12th grade who actually graduate has declined from an average 73 percent between 1977 and 1979 to 50 percent in 1984. Another consequence is that education has become a focal point of black resistance to apartheid.

The leaders of the endemic school boycotts argue that equal education is not possible without political equality and that black students ought to stay out of school until "political liberation." Many black schools have been razed in student protests.

Despite recent increases, the state spends seven times more per capita on white education than on black education. The government has committed itself to providing equal (but separate) education for all races, but it expects that it will take 10 years to close the gap between government expenditure on black and white education.

BLACK PERCEPTIONS OF THE PRIORITIES
FOR COMMUNITY DEVELOPMENT

There was general agreement among those interviewed that community development projects should focus on the root causes of the poverty-dependency cycle. Interviewees involved in community development work were critical of the piecemeal perspective of community development that concentrates on a particular area (such as housing or education), because these are popular and visible causes, without clear insight into the nature of black underdevelopment. As one put it, "Without a clear picture of the cycle of things, you are pouring money into a bottomless pit." Most of those interviewed expressed the opinion that community development programs often perpetuate dependence by failing to address the basic causes of the poverty cycle or to transfer the skills needed for self-reliance.

Interviewees raised the following considerations as influencing their perspective on the priorities for community development:

The 'holistic perspective': One interviewee suggested that donors should have a "holistic perspective" of black community development needs. In other words, priorities must be determined by a coordinated strategy aimed at bringing about "structural transformation." Community development should concentrate on addressing the fundamental causes of black deprivation rather than simply ameliorating the symptoms of deprivation within existing structures. Palliative efforts do not alter dependency and, therefore, are not likely to enjoy the political support of blacks.

Reinventing the wheel: A feature of community development in South Africa is the vast array of programs and projects, and the minimal cooperation or coordination among them. The major reasons are competition for financial resources and ideological differences.

However, interviewees noted that many community development agencies seemed determined to "reinvent the wheel" by independently tackling problems without regard for the experience and resources of established community organizations. Some explained that the uncoordinated efforts of various community development organizations generally fail to have a significant cumulative impact on the dependency cycle. Most interviewees believed that it would be more useful to facilitate collaborative efforts and to expand existing organizations, rather than create new ones. Often an outside agent can be a useful catalyst for cooperation among organizations that otherwise might not work together.

Transfer of skills: Those interviewed felt strongly that community development agencies fail to transfer their skills, and instead, in the words of one interviewee, "jealously guard their knowledge, lest they are done out of a job." Yet another interviewee put it even more succinctly, "We don't want fish, we want to be holding the fishing pole and we want to be taught how to fish." The gist of the argument is that blacks must be given the skills to develop and carry on particular community initiatives themselves. One interviewee explained that this is another dimension of the sensitivity among blacks to the perpetuation of dependency. He said "blacks believe that whites hold onto what they know, only giving as much as will ensure that blacks have to come back for more."

Multiplier effect: Because needs in South Africa far outstrip the available resources, it is important to base priorities for support on attaining the maximum benefit for the maximum number of people. The coordination of resources and a carefully planned strategy for the attainment of projected goals are important.

A sense of the long term: Many useful initiatives are hamstrung because foreign donors provide the initial "seed money" in the expectation that South Africans will provide the long term funding. Whereas South African participation should be encouraged, and it is reasonable to make funding conditional on the participation of other donors, sources of funding in South Africa are limited. Moreover, few organizations have the resources to finance fundraising trips abroad.

Furthermore, we have already noted that the problems of deprivation in South Africa will not be addressed in the short term. The implication is that a long term commitment is important to ensure the fulfillment of any community development initiative. Often the commitment of a major donor may be used to galvanize broader financial support.

Interviewees suggested that donor agencies ought to be clear about their motives for involvement in community development in South Africa. Most interviewees expressed the belief that interest in South Africa is based more on an attempt to "absolve international moral guilt" than on any philanthropic commitment. Many said they feared that once the trappings of apartheid had been dismantled international concern would wane.

What about the homelands?: A further issue is the urban-rural nexus. Whereas the rural areas are the most deprived, the migration of blacks in search of subsistence opportunities increases the pressure on the already limited resources in the urban centers. Interviewees emphasized the interrelatedness of urban and rural conditions and the need to address both dimensions of the problem. Some interviewees expressed the fear that the migration of increasing numbers of rural blacks to the cities will exacerbate the existing problems of overcrowding and unemployment in the urban areas and result in the replication of the levels of poverty and starvation common in the rural areas.

This raises the politically sensitive question of pursuing community development projects in the homelands. Those interviewed were adamant that the homelands could not be excluded because, as one interviewee put it, "These people are political prisoners who should not be further punished." However, there is absolute opposition to any association with the homeland governments. Nonetheless, some dealings with homeland authorities might be unavoidable, since they control many facets of homeland life. The homeland governments maintain a considerable network of control through their power of patronage, such as the allocation of land, the provision of housing, the provision of schools and community facilities and the payment of pensions and student scholarships, and it is seldom possible to initiate undertakings in the homeland areas without coming up against the authority of homeland administrations. Many homeland officials are corrupt, and interviewees sounded a warning against bribing officials for favors or conferring political recognition on the homeland governments.

As discussed earlier, all aspects of black disadvantage are linked in a cycle of poverty and dependence that is rooted in the political decisions of the ruling white government. However, it is also clear that a redistribution of political power will not automatically lead to an improvement in the quality of life for most blacks. The basic elements of rural black poverty are hunger, disease and the lack of basic community facilities — running water, sanitation, housing. The spillover effect of these conditions on black urban life has already been discussed. Alleviation of chronic destitution in the rural areas is fundamental to any attempt at improving the quality of life for blacks everywhere in the country.

RURAL SUBSISTENCE

At least 9 million of approximately 13 million rural blacks live below the poverty line, and about 1.4 million have no measurable income at all. At the turn of the century more than 80 percent of rural dwellers were subsistence farmers; that figure is now about 8 percent. Those who were driven off the land by the soil impoverishment and overcrowding became seasonal laborers on South Africa's white owned farms. But five years of drought and growing mechanization have led many white farmers to lay off most of their seasonal laborers and to retain only skeleton labor crews. The availability of seasonal employment, which is the major source of income for those remaining in the homelands, has shrunk by more than two-thirds since 1982.

In 1980 only about 13 percent of the homeland population was comprised of males in the economically important age group of 20 to 54. The remainder are forced by economic necessity to migrate to the metropolitan centers — increasing competition for scarce jobs and placing additional pressure on meager urban facilities. Salaries earned by migrant laborers are rarely sufficient to subsidize families remaining in the homelands. The result is a pattern of malnutrition and children's diseases that approaches the levels found in some of Africa's most destitute countries. This situation is exacerbated by the dearth of adequate health care facilities.

The annual average black infant mortality rate is about 100 per 1,000 live births — it is estimated to be double this in the rural areas — contrasted with 13.9 per 1,000 among whites. About 55 percent of deaths among blacks occur between the ages of one and five years. Average life expectancy for blacks is about 15 years less than for whites. Whites die of the diseases of Western affluence, such as heart disease; blacks of those of Third World poverty.

About one-third of South Africa's black children are chronically undernourished. According to the South African Red Cross, between 120,000 and 300,000 black children die each year from illness related to poor nutrition and the lack of basic community services. Kwashiorkor and marasmus are the two most common forms of illness resulting from undernourishment. These diseases of malnutrition are one of the four most common causes of death among black children. The others are respiratory ailments (such as pneumonia), measles and gastroenteritis.

Tuberculosis and cholera are the two most prevalent diseases in South Africa. The incidence of TB among Africans has increased by 22 percent since 1977; about 23,000 Africans have died of TB in the last 10 years. Although TB is by far the most widespread disease among Africans, sporadic cholera epidemics are common; during 1981-82 an estimated 50,000 people were infected with cholera and 200 died from the disease, although unofficial estimates put that figure much higher.

The problem of rural subsistence cannot be addressed in a piecemeal fashion. The interrelatedness of the elements contributing to rural destitution demands a coordinated approach that tackles the most fundamental aspects — hunger, community facilities and health care.

Hunger: Experts estimate that 70 percent of the supposedly arable land in the homelands is located in areas that the rest of Africa would consider marginal wasteland. Thus the prospects of large scale farming operations in these regions are limited. Moreover, land allocation in the homelands is complicated by the traditional system of land tenure, whereby land is allocated by a local tribal chief in return for a percentage of the crop yield. Furthermore, although there is a reasonable expectation of land redistribution after majority government, the vital role of white farmers in producing food to feed the whole nation will reduce the scale and pace of land reallocation to blacks. Thus the emphasis in black agricultural activity is likely to remain subsistence farming, and it is at this level that the problem of hunger should be addressed. It is not possible to launch large scale agricultural schemes in the homelands without involving the homeland authorities, but smaller, localized agricultural projects, invariably sanctioned by a local chief or village headman, are possible, and there are a number of successful examples.

An effective means of subsistence agriculture is the communal or collective model where input and yield are shared equally by community members. The key to the success of this method is effective community organization and mobilization. However, certain basic commodities such as water, seed, fertilizer and the appropriate implements are required at the outset. Moreover, this relatively intensive pattern of agricultural production requires specialized understanding of matters such as crop rotation and the replenishment of nutrients in the soil.

The cooperation of local villagers is essential to the success of any such undertaking. Rural black communities are often suspicious of outsiders, and it is therefore necessary to work through the local tribal chief or a committee of individuals nominated by a particular community. Most communities have a recognizable leadership hierarchy that is generally best able to mobilize other community members. Although positions of authority are invariably occupied by older men, because of the migration of younger men to jobs in the cities for long periods, women predominate in rural communities. It is also traditionally accepted in rural communities that women tend crops and undertake the work necessary to maintain the household.

A number of organizations are involved in the development of communal agricultural projects. Significant among these is the Black Housewives' League. This organization is made up mostly of urban black women who work to secure the resources needed by rural black women for the development of home industries and subsistence agricultural cooperatives. The Black Housewives' League is particularly active in the rural areas of the North Eastern Transvaal and often collaborates with Operation Hunger — the major private famine relief agency — in identifying communities for assistance in developing communal agricultural projects. A similar non-racial group known as Self-Help Associates for Development Economics (Shade) also provides training in self-help skills. Furthermore, the Valley Trust, which operates in the KwaZulu homeland, has been involved in the development of communal gardens and agricultural extension work in that region since 1953.

Some debate exists about whether there is a real shortfall in South Africa's food supply, but there is certainly a serious maldistribution of food supplies influenced primarily by the inability of many rural communities to purchase food. A number of agencies, such as Operation Hunger, World Vision and the Red Cross, are involved in famine relief work in areas where hunger is most severe. Many of those interviewed described the famine relief activities of these agencies as "band aid" operations and criticized them for increasing black dependency on "handouts." They were emphatic that such assistance be linked to the development of community skills of self-reliance or, as one interviewee put it, "You will have to come back again and again, and the problem will have grown worse."

Some interviewees proposed village cooperatives that buy foodstuffs in bulk at wholesale prices. Another idea was that of food warehouses, located in regional centers, where the major food supply companies would sell their products that do not meet normal consumer standards at much reduced prices to needy blacks. This concept was raised in South Africa several years ago, but has never been implemented.

Community facilities: Studies presented at a 1984 conference as part of a three year inquiry into poverty and development in Southern Africa, sponsored by Carnegie Corporation of New York, reported that in certain areas of the Eastern Transvaal there was an average of one water tap to 760 people. More than half the villages surveyed had no access to clean water at all. Similar evidence for many other rural districts indicate that this is typical. Moreover, in most rural villages there is no sanitation, houses are crudely constructed and badly ventilated, there are often few accessible roads, clinic facilities are generally a long distance away — with villagers having to travel an estimated average of 50 to 100 miles for medical care — and public transport is limited and irregular. These are major factors in the pattern of hunger and disease in South Africa.

The alleviation of black rural poverty obviously depends on the provision of basic community facilities. The most pressing need is for the provision of water boreholes, piped drinking water and water storage dams for irrigation. Signatories to the Sullivan code of employment practice for American businesses in South Africa have initiated the Rural Fulfillment Foundation. This organization is dedicated to assisting rural villagers in the provision of basic community facilities and the establishment of subsistence farming projects. The effort has been limited to a small number of villages in the Eastern Cape, the Free State and the Transvaal, but the U.S. corporate sponsors of the program are hopeful of expanding to other areas.

Health care: A key factor in addressing black rural poverty is the provision of primary health care services. The concept of the "barefoot doctor" — who is both primary health worker and community development manager — is particularly appropriate for the Third World conditions of rural South Africa, originating as it did in the rural areas of the People's Republic of China. Ideally such individuals should be nominated by their respective communities to facilitate community cooperation and mobilization and then trained in basic diagnostic skills to be able to treat common ailments. The barefoot doctor's training would also emphasize preventive health care and health education to improve nutrition, including the initiation of staple crop growing projects and improving water supply and sanitation. Because a crucial factor in the effectiveness of this type of scheme is securing the trust and confidence of the community concerned, the barefoot doctor must also be a skilled community organizer.

The function of the barefoot doctor is tied into a network of clinic and hospital facilities, as well as community development resource centers. In the event of drought or crop failure, for example, it is the task of the barefoot doctor to mobilize famine relief before starvation sets in.

This is the ideal model. In practice there are a number of constraints, mostly arising from the lack of a primary health care system in South Africa and the traditional emphasis on a curative rather than preventive health service. Moreover, there are a number of disparate private initiatives aimed at providing primary health care for remote communities, but these are mostly run by university medical schools, and insufficient attention is given to the developmental function of the primary health care worker.

A number of interviewees argued that until there is change in the focus of national health policy it would not be possible to implement a genuine primary health care system. Others argued that if a primary health care system could be developed with private funds this would ultimately change national health policy. Proponents of both arguments agreed, however, that the barefoot doctor concept is the ideal for which private initiatives aimed at alleviating black rural poverty should reach.

National health policy: Separate health care facilities are provided for whites, Africans, coloreds and Asians — including separate hospitals, clinics and ambulances. White health care services are generally rated on a par with those of most industrialized countries, while black services range from the rudimentary in urban areas to almost non-existent in many rural areas.

The government spends on aggregate four times more on health care for whites than for blacks. The percentage of gross national product spent on health care has declined from 4.2 percent in 1976 to approximately 3 percent in 1986. About 7 percent of the government's annual budget is spent on health care and only about 3 percent of the health care budget is devoted to preventive care.

There are about 44,000 hospital beds available for whites, a ratio of 102:1, and a total of 77,542 hospital beds for blacks, a ratio of 337:1 for Africans, 500:1 for Asians and 346:1 for coloreds. Hospital expenditure per patient averages $15 for Africans and $45 for whites. Using the formula of one hospital bed for every 250 people, it is estimated that there is an oversupply of 9,000 beds for whites and a shortfall of 17,000 beds for blacks. The average bed occupancy rate in white hospitals is 59 percent, as against 95.2 percent in black hospitals.

There are about 20,000 medical doctors in South Africa, of whom 500 are Africans. This represents a total doctor to population ratio of about 1:750 in urban areas, but in rural areas the ratio is about 1:25,000. In some areas the ratio is as high as one doctor to 44,000 people. Only about 5 percent of all South African doctors work in rural areas.

According to the World Health Organization, developing countries need at least two registered nurses per 1,000 people in order to render a basic health service. In South Africa there are only 1.5 nurses per 1,000 Africans as against six registered nurses per 1,000 whites. African nurses are paid about 30 percent less than their white counterparts. Black nurses are barred from caring for white patients, and white nurses may not work in hospitals for blacks.

Of the approximately 1,000 medical doctors graduating from medical schools each year, about 7 percent are Africans, 2 percent are coloreds and 10 percent are Asians. The failure rate among black medical students ranges between 25 and 50 percent. There are four medical schools in South Africa that admit blacks as students: the Medical University of Southern Africa (Medunsa), the University of Natal, the University of Cape Town and the University of the Witwatersrand.

About 60 health professionals graduate from Medunsa, outside Pretoria, each year.

Because Medunsa was set up specifically to provide medical training for blacks, many blacks see it as a creation of apartheid and suspect that the training is not on a par with that of white medical schools. The medical schools attached to white universities graduate far fewer blacks — although the Universities of Cape Town and the Witwatersrand have instituted remedial tuition programs to bring potential black students up to their high enrollment standards. The University of the Witwatersrand has succeeded in increasing the number of black students from 10 to 70 since 1985.

Perceptions of an alternative health care system: Many interviewees argued that the foundations of a health care system that seeks to ensure "health for all" will rest not so much on physical facilities and curative services, but on the health professionals trained to provide preventive services. All agreed that "health for all" could not be achieved simply by upgrading and extending existing facilities and that, as one explained, "Unless there are vast improvements made in nutrition, housing and health education, the mere provision of more 'doctoring' will not lead to any real improvement in public health."

In general terms, interviewees spoke of the increasingly popular focus among developmentalists on community based health services. They agreed that:

— health care projects should be based on maximum community participation;
— the emphasis should be on preventive services such as health education;
— the emphasis should fall on the training of a large number of primary health care workers;
— these primary health care workers should constitute the key element in a developmental approach to the eradication of black rural poverty.

Proponents of the primary health care approach argue that it is unrealistic to rely on doctors to provide the backbone of a primary health care system for the following reasons:

— it would be impossible to train enough doctors rapidly enough to meet the projected needs;
— medical schools are controlled by specialists and provide inappropriate training to their young doctors to meet the primary health needs of the community;
— doctors generally adopt an elitist attitude and are often far removed from the societies they serve;
— doctors avoid working in rural areas and poorer communities;
— doctors demand too high an income.

They argue that priority must be given to the training of primary health care workers. A primary health care worker ought ideally to be a woman with general nursing and midwifery qualifications and experience in clinics and hospitals. Women are more effective because rural communities are comprised mostly of women, since men are largely migrant laborers.

The aim is to equip these nurses with the clinical skills they require to diagnose and treat the vast majority of patients and to refer to a doctor those patients they are unable to treat, to understand the social and economic causes of disease and consequently to adopt a supportive and understanding attitude to their patients, the ability to manage and run a clinic, and the ability and willingness to support and assist community initiatives aimed at improving social and economic conditions, such as crop cultivation and home industries.

Some argue against taking nurses out of the hospital system where their skills are in short supply, maintaining that primary health care workers should be trained from scratch. They argue that this approach is preferable since individuals could be put forward by their respective communities for training as primary health care workers and return to their communities after training.

The ideal primary health care system envisages an interlocking network of primary health care clinics and referral hospitals. There is debate, however, about whether priority should be given to the building of primary health clinics or whether mobile clinics are more effective in serving a larger number of people at a lower cost. Proponents of permanent clinic facilities argue that the clinic should become a permanent part of the community and should not simply be there one or two days a week. They argue that mobile clinics might be a good interim measure, but that in the long run they are less effective in "upfront health care delivery" than a permanent facility.

Whereas there is consensus that the development of a primary health care system would be the most effective way of extending health care to the most disadvantaged sectors of the population and that such a system could form the basis of a national health program, there is very little coordination between individuals and institutions who share this goal. Although most are vague about the reasons, it seems that the prime causes are competition for scarce financial resources, differences in ideological and political perceptions, and protection of "academic turf" — for example, each university confines its rural health programs to an agreed homeland area and there is little sharing of resources.

The efforts of community organizations are also regionally fragmented mainly as a result of the organizational difficulties in maintaining a national network. Moreover, there is very little collaboration between academic, research and training institutions and community initiated organizations. Furthermore, academic institutions commit a lot of their time to galvanizing community involvement in their selected projects instead of relying on existing black community organizations to perform this function.

Several of the interviewees emphasized the need to concentrate on supporting research into a national health policy that encourages collaborative efforts with individuals and institutions in other countries. The experiences of Third World countries are considered the most instructive.

Where to start?: An umbrella for "progressive health care" is the National Medical and Dental Association (Namda). This organization was formed in 1982 and represents about 1,000 "progressive" doctors, dentists and medical and dental students. It is committed to "opposing apartheid in health and striving for a just and democratic society in which health for all will be a social priority." The participation and concurrence of Namda in any initiative in the field of health care is essential. Although individual Namda members might be involved in specific projects, the role of the association would be principally advisory and consultative. There is also a national Health Workers' Association representing black community health workers, black nurses and black primary health care workers.

The Department of Community Health at the University of the Witwatersrand stands out among others in the development of training programs for primary health care workers and research into alternative health systems and policy. The Department founded a Health Services Development Unit (HSDU) five years ago with the purpose of providing primary health care to rural communities in the Eastern Transvaal by training primary health care nurses.

The training for primary health care nurses consists of a one year program of academic tuition and practical experience in clinics and hospitals. The students are all qualified nurses. The HSDU will have trained 60 primary health care nurses by the end of 1986. The HSDU graduates are practicing in clinics and outpatient departments throughout the Northern and Eastern Transvaal. Moreover, the HSDU had recently expanded its program to make provision for the training of selected primary health care nurses as trainers.

Although professional and academic institutions have an important role to play in coordinating training and research, liaison with rural communities should be initiated through black community organizations that have experience in this field. Few of these organizations have a national network, and it is advisable to evaluate the most effective and credible organization in each particular region — such as the Black Housewives' League in the Transvaal or the Trust for Christian Outreach and Education, based in Pietermarizburg. In the Western Cape, the Students' Health and Welfare Centers Organization (Shawco) — a non-racial organization affiliated with the University of Cape Town — is involved in coordinating health services for local communities.

A Washington based organization known as Medical Education for South African Blacks (Mesab) has recently been established to channel U.S. funds into scholarships for the training of black South African health professionals.

If the aim is a developmental approach to alleviating black rural poverty based on the concept of a combination of primary health care and community development management — to eliminate poor nutrition and disease, and improve community facilities — the strategy ought to involve academic and professional institutions, as well as a network of appropriate black community organizations.

EDUCATION

The inequalities in black education are a result of more than three decades of "bantu" education, inadequate and overcrowded school facilities, and the underqualification and shortage of black teachers. In addition, the country's university facilities were closed to blacks in 1959 so that separate black institutions could be established in the homelands. Education's pivotal role in the oppression of blacks has made it a key issue in the black liberation struggle and a highly politicized arena.

While most of those interviewed agreed that education is fundamental to black advancement and to providing the skills needed by a majority government, all argued that change in the black education system required political action. They noted that black students have given up hoping that political action will come from the goverment or from teachers and parents. Instead, they have taken the law into their own hands and decided that they will "liberate" themselves.

This development spurred the creation of the National Education Crisis Committee, in December 1985, to coordinate the involvement of teachers, students and parents in redesigning the black education system for what it calls "people's education." This is the first time that cooperation among these three groups has been possible, and although no clear conception of "people's education" has yet been formulated, the importance of this initiative is the commitment of all three groups to take education into their own hands. Leaders of the NECC interviewed by IRRC expressed confidence that blacks would be able to "appropriate the education system."

Although, there is the clear possibility that the NECC will be obstructed by state repression, this organization has the highest degree of political legitimacy among blacks and its support of any educational initiative is crucial.

It is difficult to escape government influence and control in the educational field. A maze of 14 bureaucratic departments oversees education — one each for whites, coloreds and Indians, one for black education in "white" South Africa and one in each of the 10 homelands. As a result it is virtually impossible to undertake any initiative within formal education without the intervention of the government. Blacks, however, are strongly averse to involving government officials.

Blacks advocate support instead for private educational initiatives that, as far as possible, remain outside the structures of formal state education. They argue that working within state structures lends legitimacy to the government's separate education policy. Any private initiative in education that aspires to gain support from blacks must have as its aim the transformation of the existing educational system, not only to provide equal education for all, but to reflect black aspirations.

Pre-school education: Pre-schooling among blacks in South Africa is important in ensuring school readiness. Most black mothers in the urban areas have to work, and children are left from a very early age in the care of an aged relative or older children who are not in school. The result is a high level of malnutrition and neglect that impairs physical and mental development.

One of the best known private initiatives is the Grassroots Education Trust in the Western Cape, which aims at improving the facilities and nutrition available to pre-school children. The Early Learning Resource Unit, also based in Cape Town, provides in-service training for pre-school teachers in disadvantaged communities. Furthermore, the Western Cape Foundation for Community Work provides administrative and professional support to community initiated day care centers for pre-school children. Similar services are provided in Soweto by the Entokozweni Early Learning and Community Services Center. The Center for Social Development, located at Grahamstown in the Eastern Cape, is responsible for the development of pre-school institutions in that region.

Primary and secondary education: Unlike that for other population groups, education for Africans is compulsory only in those few areas where there are sufficient school facilities, and the time which an African child spends at school is generally a function of economics. Few African families can afford to keep children at school unless there are sufficient breadwinners, and thus older children often have to subsidize the education of siblings. More than 50 percent of African students drop out of school before they reach the fourth grade.

Although the percentage of Africans graduating from high school is declining, the absolute number of graduates is increasing. A key factor in the high dropout rate and low standard of African schooling is the rapid expansion of school enrollments. The number of black pupils increased from 800,000 in 1950 to 5 million in 1985. There are not enough qualified teachers or adequate facilities to produce successful results. The average pupil to teacher ratio in the urban areas is 40:1 for blacks as opposed to 18:1 for whites. Moreover, approximately 70 percent of African pupils are in the homelands where the pupil to teacher ratio averages 90:1. Nearly 75 percent of black teachers do not have the minimum teaching qualifications. More than 50 percent of black pupils that make it to the 12th grade will fail to graduate.

A 1984 survey by the South African Institute of Race Relations among Soweto students revealed that 40 percent of those surveyed did not have a teacher for all subjects at school, 41 percent did not have textbooks for all their school subjects, 5 percent had 70 to 80 pupils in their class at school and 52 percent did not have access to a library. It found that 72 percent lived in a four room house and 36 percent did not have electricity at home — making it difficult for them to study in the evenings.

Most interviewees argued that although primary education is in as poor a state as secondary education, the education system should be revamped from the top down to allow more senior students to have the immediate benefit of improvements in education. Others argued that unless the school system was reformed from the foundation up, secondary school students would continue to reflect the weaknesses of their early education. Nonetheless, most interviewees agreed that the main focus should be on remedial education to enable more blacks to graduate from school, since students must pass a state approved exam to be admitted to any South African university. No alternatives to the state exam exist at the moment — although some universities are contemplating other admission criteria — and hence much of the energy in private education initiatives is aimed at preparing students for it.

Moreover, students in many regions of the country have been boycotting classes sporadically, and in some areas continuously, for almost three years, causing the black school system in areas such as the Eastern Cape and parts of Pretoria and the Johannesburg area to collapse. Thus interviewees focused on the need to provide alternative educational opportunities — outside of the state system — for these students.

Alternative education: A number of organizations aim to provide remedial and alternative educational opportunities in different parts of the country. Two of the best known black run organizations are the South African Committee for Higher Education (Sached) and the Johannesburg-based University Preparation Program (UPP).

Sached has active branches in all regions of the country and is the largest of the agencies working in the field of alternative education. Sached provides course materials and instruction aimed at remedying the shortcomings in the state system. The UPP, on the other hand, is a special tutorial program aimed at the preparation of students for the state school leaving exam. The UPP has recently established a study center in Johannesburg to provide remedial instruction for 11th and 12th grade students.

The most ambitious endeavor to date has been the creation by Sached of Khanya College — a collaborative initiative with Indiana University aimed at upgrading the academic skills of black students to enable them to compete at the open universities.

The program was launched in 1986. Although it now only admits students for one year of study preparatory to acceptance at established tertiary institutions, the aim is for Khanya to develop into South Africa's first private college. Khanya College has residential campuses in Johannesburg and Cape Town.

Private primary and secondary schools: There are a large number of private primary and secondary schools in South Africa, most of which have denominational affiliations, and even though many receive small state subsidies, they do not depend on the state for funding, and thus they have been able to maintain traditionally more liberal admissions policies and curricula than state run schools. The number of black pupils enrolled at private schools has increased significantly in the last 10 years because of the sporadic disruption of public schools for blacks. Private schools charge tuition fees that few blacks can afford to pay, but increasing numbers of blacks are attending private schools. This fact is the cause of some controversy in the black community because community activists argue that these pupils are failing in their duty to the liberation struggle by attending school while their less affluent "brothers" are boycotting classes.

Interviewees' opinions were divided between those who see the private school system as offering a model for non-racial education, and those who perceive these institutions as providing elitist education that will further divide the black community. The latter group do not see private schools as a viable alternative to the state run schools and believe that focusing on private schools detracts attention from the unequal and discriminatory nature of schooling for most blacks. In contrast, the former group take the view that private schools offer blacks a superior education and those who can should attend them. Obviously scholarships for black students to attend private schools would increase the number of blacks able to take advantage of this opportunity.

There are various associations of private schools in different parts of the country that would be well placed to administer scholarships for this purpose. A number of black educationists mentioned the New Era Schools Trust (Nest) — a private initiative by black and white educationists to build non-racial schools in different parts of the country — as a useful development. The first of the Nest schools is under construction at Tongaat on the Natal North Coast. Others are planned for the Eastern Cape and the Transvaal.

The American Chamber of Commerce in South Africa financed the development of a private black secondary school in Soweto known as Pace College. The first students were due to graduate at the end of 1985, but the school has become a political target and has been temporarily closed. Interviewees suggested a number of reasons for the forced closure of Pace College: It was not racially integrated, it taught principally commercial subjects (which some activists argued prepared students only to serve the corporate sponsors of the school), it had failed after five years of operation to appoint a black headmaster, and it maintained close links with the government's department for African education. Interviewees pointed to examples of other private schools that have a majority of black students, such as St. Barnabas College in Bosmont — a colored township outside Johannesburg — but have not elicited political censure from the black community because, interviewees argued, they are seen to be clearly separate from the structure of apartheid education.

Few private schools are located in black townships, and thus most are not as vulnerable to black student protests as Pace College. However, black student organizations have also demanded the withdrawal of black students from private schools in white areas. At a meeting of the NECC and private school headmasters in September 1986, student leaders accused the private schools of providing a haven for black students running away from the struggle, of promoting elitism and perpetuating class differences. On the other hand, black educationists at the meeting argued that private schools should work to become truly non-racial institutions and have an important role to play in shaping an education system more appropriate to the interests of the majority of South Africans.

Career guidance: An additional factor in the poor standard of black education is the inappropriate combination of academic skills with which most students graduate. Often students are unaware that specific subjects such as mathematics are a prerequisite for university admission. Moreover, many find that their schooling does not qualify them for admission to any tertiary institution and that their career options are severely restricted — "so they are shunted into the mainstream of black labor," in the words of one black educationist.

Career guidance for black students is a recent phenomenon. Over the last 10 years, privately run career guidance centers have been established in the black townships of the major urban centers, of which the largest are the Soweto Career Center near Johannesburg and the Careers Research and Information Center (CRIC) in Cape Town. The Education Information Center (EIC) in Johannesburg serves as a resource agency for many local career centers and also has a skills testing and job placement service.

A number of career centers, as well as the regional branches of the South African Council of Churches, run "winter schools" during the July school vacation to provide remedial education for senior black students.

Learning facilities: There are more than 12,000 schools for blacks, the majority of which lack even rudimentary facilities such as electricity and sanitation. Unlike white schools, most black schools do not have playing fields or sports facilities, and very few have libraries or science labs.

Two streams of thought on the merits of upgrading black school facilities emerged from the interviews. Some argued that sophisticated facilities would not contribute to change in the content of black education, but as one interviewee said "simply puts a glossy wrapper round it." Proponents of this argument do not deny the dearth of learning and teaching facilities such as science labs and libraries, but they are of the opinion that improving facilities is not the first priority. Others argued that the lack of learning facilities is a significant factor in the poor performance of black students and that upgrading these facilities would increase the number of blacks graduating from high school and improve their opportunities for further study.

These arguments aside, state-run schools are the target of black student protests. Many of these schools have been completely razed, and most others have been damaged by arson and other forms of destruction. Few private schools have been known to incur such damage.

The largest private initiative to upgrade black school facilities is the Adopt-A-School program launched in 1978 by signatories to the Sullivan code of employment practices for U.S. firms in South Africa. A 1985 survey of this program commissioned by IRRC revealed mixed attitudes among black students and teachers. Black students saw no real benefit in the program, maintaining that the improvements were mostly to the facilities for teachers. Students were of the opinion that improving facilities is a ploy to make them more accepting of "bantu" education. Teachers, on the other hand, were generally in favor of the program, but most commented that it contributed little to their skills as teachers or to the general quality of black education.

A related program, Read — which aims to provide black schools with library material — was more severely criticized by interviewees for its close association with the Department of Education and Training (DET), which is responsible for African education. Interviewees argued that the books Read provided to black schools had to be approved by the DET, and as a result only "bantu education material is provided," as one prominent black educationist put it. Black teachers and pupils interviewed by IRRC pointed out that these libraries were often no more than a shelf of books that was hopelessly inadequate for the large number of pupils at most black schools, that often teaching staff lacked any idea of how to administer the libraries and that in a short period of time most of the books would disappear. Furthermore, some black pupils said activists had deliberately burnt library books because they thought they had been placed in the schools by the DET. All interviewees agreed that there is a desperate need for library facilities for blacks, but said these should be entirely independent of government-related institutions.

Teacher upgrading programs: Not only are most black teachers underqualified, but the black school population is expected to double in the next 15 years with the result that government planners estimate that an additional 12,000 teachers in black schools will be required each year. At present only 6,000 black teacher candidates graduate each year, and two-thirds of them have less than the minimum graduate qualifications required for teachers.

A number of private initiatives exist to upgrade the qualifications and teaching competence of black teachers. The largest of these endeavors is the Teacher Opportunities Program (TOPS), sponsored principally by Mobil Oil, which has been particularly active in the Eastern and Western Cape and the Johannesburg area. Sached also runs programs in its various regional centers to prepare teachers for the school leaving exam.

Interviewees questioned about the merits of teacher upgrading programs were generally cynical. Most argued that many private institutions and corporations have seized on teacher upgrading as the panacea for the "black school problem." Since blacks are primarily opposed to the content of black education, they argue that until the content changes black schools will continue to produce inept teachers. One educationist said, "Of course we need better qualified teachers, but it is a Catch 22 situation" because inferior black schooling perpetuates the poor educational grounding of black teachers. Black students interviewed said they thought teachers joined teacher upgrading programs so that they could claim a higher salary, but there had been no noticeable improvement in the standard of teaching. Many decried the fact that teachers were removed from classrooms to participate in upgrading programs during school hours and that students were often left to fend for themselves.

Adult education: The inadequacy of the formal schooling system and the demands of the economy for more skilled workers has created a considerable demand for non-formal education. After decades of mother-tongue or vernacular instruction under bantu education, blacks' competence in English — the principal medium of communication — is generally poor. Furthermore, there is a high level of illiteracy among blacks. According to a 1983 report of the South African President's Council, 50 percent of all South Africans over 20 years of age are illiterate. Some 68 percent of adult Africans are unable to read or write; 52 percent of urban and 79 percent of rural Africans are illiterate.

Blacks are mostly "underemployed" insofar as they are often consigned to jobs well below their aptitudes because they have received inadequate education. Interviewees gave high priority to general skills training aimed at improving the "life opportunities" of blacks doing menial jobs. The same problem exists in the under utilization of black managers in the corporate sector. Only 2 percent of all managers in the private sector are blacks. At current manpower requirements there is a need to advance 4,000 blacks into management positions each year, yet fewer than 500 black managers are now appointed annually.

There is a great need for what is often referred to as "second chance" education, and the demand is expected to increase considerably as more blacks have their education disrupted by political upheaval. The point of "second chance" education, as the name suggests, is to give adults the opportunity of upgrading their school qualifications.

Interviewees were enthusiastic about the idea that non-formal education offered real opportunities to improve the level of black education in advance of a fundamental change in the quality of black schooling. Many pointed to the fact that non-formal education takes place outside of the government education structures and, therefore, literally knows no bounds. However, some interviewees sounded a note of criticism of the content of several private non-formal training programs that aimed only at providing skills for menial jobs — such as domestic service.

Non-formal education is mostly in private hands, and the largest private agency is the South African Committee for Higher Education (Sached). Sached is involved in a variety of adult education programs, including organizational training for black unionists and community workers, and second chance education programs.

Technical training: Education for blacks, because it concentrates almost exclusively on academic subjects, does not equip graduates with the technical skills increasingly needed for jobs in an industrial economy.

There are only three government-sponsored institutions for the advanced technical training of Africans — the Mabopane East Technikon outside Pretoria, under the control of the Department of Education and Training, and the Mangosothu Technikon and Edendale College in KwaZulu under the KwaZulu Department of Education. In the four independent homelands, however, there are a number of tertiary technical training institutions. Moreover, there are a number of privately funded technical training institutions, mostly established by business organizations to provide vocational training, such as the training center supported by the motor industry in Port Elizabeth.

Since the removal of restrictions on black job mobility in the late 1970s, blacks increasingly have advanced into skilled jobs. This advancement is the prime reason for the marginal redistribution of income from white to black that has occurred over the last decade. The demand for skilled blacks is likely to continue to increase, and most interviewees agreed that access to technical training for blacks is an important priority. Some educationists argued that the focus should be on the establishment of more secondary schools that concentrate on technical education because school graduates often lack even a basic grasp of technical concepts.

An important issue is the relationship between education and unemployment. Outside of industry there are few opportunities for the training of blacks in skills such as plumbing, bricklaying and car repairs that enable people to go into business for themselves.

University education: All universities, both black and white, are public institutions in that they are established by statute and receive approximately 85 percent of their funding from the state. In 1959, the government created four new universities for blacks — the University of the Western Cape for coloreds, the University of Durban-Westville for Asians, the University of the North and the University of Zululand for Africans — alongside the already established University of Fort Hare for Africans. Blacks were to be permitted to study at white universities only if they qualified for special government exemption.

The white English language universities — the Universities of Cape Town, Natal and the Witwatersrand, and Rhodes University — consistently opposed the exclusion of black students and over the years succeeded in increasing black enrollment. As a result, these universities are generally referred to as the "open universities." In 1983, the government relaxed the restriction on black admissions to white universities on condition that blacks did not exceed 15 percent of the annual student enrollment. Some universities have already exceeded this quota and have expressed their determination to continue to increase the number of black students on campus. The average enrollment of black students at the open universities consequently increased from less than 10 percent before 1983 to more than 15 percent in 1985. An average of 20 percent of the black students enrolled at the "open universities" are Africans; the other 80 percent are coloreds and Asians.

Although the black universities are variously described as "bush colleges" and "tribal universities," these institutions are the most accessible for the majority of black students. Educationists said that the Universities of the North, Zululand and Fort Hare are generally rated lowest by African students for a number of reasons: Academic faculty are said to be mainly professors who are unable to get posts at more prestigious schools, Afrikaners predominate on the faculty, and the administration is viewed as reactionary and pro-government. As a result, these institutions are subject to frequent student strikes.

The University of Fort Hare is situated in the nominally independent homeland of Ciskei. This homeland government is particularly repressive, and university faculty and students are regular government targets. The other three independent homelands — Transkei, Venda and Bophuthatswana — also have university campuses established after "independence." Of these three, only the University of Bophuthatswana has established a credible academic reputation, although it too has recently been the scene of political disruption.

All black universities were recently granted "autonomy" — the right, long held by white universities, to appoint high level administrators, to establish new academic programs, to raise funds for new facilities and to determine admissions criteria irrespective of race.

The University of Durban-Westville and the University of the Western Cape have been able to establish far more solid academic reputations. Although created on the same basis as other black universities, they have grown increasingly independent over the years. The University of the Western Cape has gone furthest in improving the quality of faculty, establishing non-racial admissions criteria and lessening dependence on state control and funding, and it was often cited by interviewees as the best example of a school that is being reformed from within to meet black aspirations.

Blacks interviewed by IRRC expressed the view that although the origin of the "tribal universities" in the racist ideology of apartheid was repugnant, the majority of African students have no option but to enroll at these institutions. Therefore, while some argued that supporting the "tribal universities" would lend credibility to the government's separate education policy, others were of the opinion that more black students would derive benefit from an improvement in standards at black segregated institutions. The improvement mentioned most often was upgrading black faculty to a level of academic competence akin to that at colleges in the United Kingdom and the United States. By contrast, the role of the open universities was seen by most of those interviewed as somewhat controversial.

The open universities still remain inaccessible to most black students because of the high cost of tuition compared with that of the black universities and because of the rigorous admission standards applied by these institutions. The open universities have responded with scholarship programs and remedial education and orientation courses for black students, but black students often perceive these support services as evidence that the university views them as inferior to white students.

The general view is that the open universities are essentially white institutions that profess liberal attitudes, but are racially discriminatory both in their admission of students and in the advancement of faculty. A number of interviewees pointed to the fact that there are only two black faculty with the rank of professor at the University of the Witwatersrand. As one interviewee put it, "Until these universities are Africanized at the top level, the institutional momentum ensures that they remain white." Furthermore, interviewees bemoaned the fact that a very small percentage of the black students are Africans. They argued that in the past the open universities could have been far more vigorous in their opposition to government-enforced restrictions on the enrollment of black students, but that the universities had been intimidated by the government's threat to withdraw state subsidies. Although some acknowledged the efforts now being made by the open universities to increase black enrollment, others said the admissions criteria excluded most blacks because of their weak school education.

Interviewees explained that most black students find themselves at a disadvantage in the predominantly white culture of the open universities. White administrators at the University of the Witwatersrand and the University of Cape Town admitted that these charges had some validity, but confirmed their commitment to becoming fully non-racial institutions. The University of Cape Town in particular has embarked on rigorous efforts to "Africanize" the campus, both through an affirmative student admissions policy and through a faculty advancement program. Black faculty members interviewed at the University of Cape Town said that a great deal had yet to be done, but they thought the university leaders' commitment sincere.

Some black educationists charge the open universities with "academic imperialism" insofar as they are perceived to be trying to impose their model of education based on British and American educational traditions on all other universities, and those that do not conform appear to both black students and potential donors as substandard. These educationists argue that this places the black universities and thus most black students at a disadvantage. They noted that just as blacks demanded "people's education" in secondary schools, they would expect black universities to reflect the educational and philosophical aspirations of black South Africans. With this end in mind, they suggested that the existing black universities should be developed into colleges to provide bridging education between secondary schools and the existing prestigious open universities.

A broad consensus emerged on the question of priorities for support by donor agencies. All interviewees agreed that the lack of funds is the principal restriction on black university enrollment. However, there are different views about the priority that should be given to scholarships for overseas study, for enrollment at the open universities or for attending black universities.

Scholarships for overseas study: Many interviewees argued that the cost of overseas study is disproportionately high and that many more scholarships for study in South Africa could be provided for the same money. Others, while not disagreeing with the economics of the argument, were of the opinion that the "psychologically liberating" experience of overseas study is invaluable. They point to the fact that black South Africans generally attain much greater academic success at foreign universities than at domestic institutions. At the same time, there was agreement that the academic training provided by foreign institutions is not always appropriate to the South African job market. Interviewees argued that South Africa is for the most part a Third World country that needs the skills appropriate to a developing economy, and they maintained that overseas education raises the danger of an oversupply of inappropriately qualified black graduates.

The Educational Opportunities Council (EOC) is the organization responsible for the selection of the bulk of black students studying in the United States and Europe. Most of the remaining scholarships for overseas study are administered by the South African Institute of Race Relations. The EOC is affiliated with the New York-based South African Education Program (SAEP) — a four way initiative by American universities, major American philanthropies, the American business sector and the U.S. government to provide educational opportunities in the United States for black South Africans. The SAEP is administered by the Institute of International Education (IIE) in New York. Officers of the EOC interviewed by IRRC pointed to the fact that all returning students to date had been successfully placed in jobs. They are particularly proud of the fact that although a number of students stay on in the United States for further study, more than 95 percent return to South Africa on completion of their studies. Moreover, only nine of the 290 students in the United States between 1979 and 1985 returned without an academic qualification.

A recent evaluation of the program commissioned by the SAEP came to the following conclusions:

— Students were adequately equipped for study at U.S. colleges and universities.
— In general, students responded successfully to the challenges of a foreign system of higher education and built highly satisfactory academic records.
— Students reported that exposure to courses, readings and technology that were unavailable to them in South Africa had expanded their knowledge base significantly.
— Students cited increased self-confidence, an increased sense of intellectual competence and greater self-assurance as psychological benefits of U.S. study.
— Most scholarship recipients, upon returning to South Africa, found positions that were commensurate with their training and compatible with their career objectives.

Approximately 1,600 applications are received each year for the 115 scholarships for overseas study administered by the EOC. Preference is given to undergraduate studies in the technical sciences or to post-graduate study. Annual selections for scholarships administered by the EOC are made by local selection panels in all major regions of the country. The selection panels also include two American academics nominated by the SAEP.

The South African Institute of Race Relations (SAIRR), which administers the remaining overseas scholarships for black students, is more controversial. Most interviewees described it as a white-run liberal institution for which blacks historically have had little regard, and they decried the lack of credible black participation in the selection process. A number of interviewees explained that there is the general perception among blacks that donors appoint the SAIRR rather than the EOC to administer scholarships because they want to avoid supporting radical students and they believe that the influence of leading black political figures who serve as trustees of the EOC, such as Archbishop Desmond Tutu, precludes the EOC from selecting politically moderate students.

Although reports that either the SAIRR or the EOC discriminates against candidates on the basis of political conviction are difficult to verify, the suspicion that this is the case is strongly held by Inkatha loyalists and some black consciousness groups. These suspicions are based mostly on perceptions of political bias in the composition of selection panels.

Scholarships for domestic study: Proponents of scholarships for domestic study reason that most black students have no alternative to study in South Africa, and therefore local institutions would be enriched by enrolling the best black students rather than sending them out of the country. Furthermore, there is a parallel argument against the concentration of scholarships for blacks at the open universities. While it is acknowledged that the "best and the brightest" should have the opportunity of studying at the "Harvards of Africa," the benefits are seen to be limited to an elitist few to the exclusion of the majority, who are restricted by a lack of funds and poor schooling to enrollment at black universities.

Interviewees repeatedly emphasized that scholarships for study at the "tribal universities" should not be "written off" because, despite their many drawbacks, those schools are a more integral part of the black community than the open universities.

41

Black educationists noted that students at black universities are likely to have their academic careers disrupted by political protest. The result is a high probability that they will take several years more than the prescribed period of study to graduate. The terms and conditions of scholarships for domestic study need to be sufficiently flexible to allow for this situation.

Strong support was voiced for the idea of providing scholarships for study by black South Africans at the universities of neighboring countries. It was pointed out that not only would this be more cost effective than overseas study, but the educational environment and the focus of education would be more appropriate to Africa and the aspirations of black South Africans. Many interviewees extolled the value of experiencing at first hand the challenges of political liberation and expressed the opinion that "the debate in Africa among Africans" is far more important to the future of black South Africans than exposure to the United States or Europe. As one interviewee put it, "South Africans know more about America than the rest of Africa. We have got to learn from the mistakes of our brothers and we can only do that if we are part of the experience."

The University of Zimbabwe in particular offers the advantage of a solid academic reputation as well as a "politically liberated" environment. The University of Botswana and the University of Lesotho at Roma are also academically reputable. However, there is some resistance on the part of these institutions to enrolling large numbers of South African students for fear that they might occupy places that otherwise could be filled by local students. Moreover, none of these universities is in a position to offer financial support to South African students.

Upgrading black universities: The principal restriction on the development of the black universities is the lack of academically competent black faculty. Interviewees advocated a coordinated program to recruit black faculty and to enhance their academic competence through post-graduate study and exposure to sophisticated educational and training techniques. There was agreement that black professors could learn a great deal about teaching methods at American educational institutions, as well as a feeling that black faculty should be given the opportunity to teach at foreign institutions so that they can be exposed to students from different educational and political environments.

The Educational Opportunities Council administers a research and teaching fellowship progam for black academics recently instituted by the University of Illinois and Northwestern University. Six fellowships are awarded annually. They provide for a term of nearly five months in the United States. A consortium of American West Coast universities, headed by the University of California state system, has recently initiated a program of mid-career, non-degree internships for black South Africans. Another group of American universities coordinated by Carnegie Corporation of New York plans to launch a similar scheme in 1987.

In addition to these programs, there is a need to train black university administrators to replace the government appointees currently responsible for the administration of most black universities. Again advanced training and learning experiences at overseas institutions would be appropriate. The idea of shorter internships, where black university administrators work for a time in the administration of an overseas educational institution, was cited as particularly useful.

However, interviewees argued strongly that although there are "progressive pockets" deserving of support at several black universities, "blanket" support should not be given to any black university until the institution is firmly set on an independent course. They maintained that while giving money to a black university would lessen the institution's dependence on the state subsidy, in the eyes of blacks it is "letting the government off the hook" and lending credence to the government's separate education policy. The argument is that "the change must come from within" the individual universities before any blanket commitment can be made to help in transforming the "bush colleges" into reputable educational institutions. In the interim, assistance should be directed at individual black faculty and "progressive initiatives" within the black university system.

Training for majority government: A number of interviewees spoke of the need to encourage young black graduates to undertake post-graduate study in areas that would prepare them for senior posts in a majority government, such as public administration, urban planning and agricultural economics. They pointed out that the stability of a majority government will depend largely on administrative continuity and that few skilled black bureaucrats are "waiting in the wings." It was suggested that such training should combine academic course work with practical training in such areas as public policy formulation and analysis, urban planning and management, and financial management. Interviewees stressed that a compatible training experience is important, and some expressed doubt that American or European institutions could offer appropriate insights into African problems. Zimbabwe was mentioned as a preferable alternative.

A possible model for future programs is the Institute for Social and Economic Research at Rhodes University in the Eastern Cape, which has recently launched a post-graduate course for the training of blacks in international affairs and foreign policy formulation. The aim is to provide a foundation course for the training of would-be black diplomats.

JOB CREATION

An additional 350,000 new job seekers will enter the market each year over the next 14 years, requiring more than 1,000 new jobs each day if new entrants into the job market are to be accommodated. Even at optimistic official estimates of an average 3.5 percent economic growth rate, by the year 2000 unemployment among Africans will officially top 40 percent. In reality that figure is likely to exceed 50 percent.

South Africa has experienced negative economic growth in four of the last five years, and continued political instability, the low ebb of international investor confidence and international pressure to isolate the South African economy make the prospects for a short term improvement remote. Large scale retrenchment of black workers — particularly in the manufacturing sector — has taken place over the last two years. According to the government statistical service, an average of 8,000 jobs were lost each month during 1985.

Sustained economic growth and increasing foreign investment are the principal motors of job creation in South Africa. However, job creation is a complex problem in that society, in part because foreign investment is at the center of political pressure aimed at the demise of white government in South Africa. Most of those interviewed agreed that economic disruption — through disinvestment, consumer boycotts and industrial action — is the only peaceful strategy open to blacks to pressure whites to surrender political power. They recognized, however, that unemployment and job creation will be among the most pressing problems facing a majority government.

Although most agreed that some foreign investors would be welcomed back after majority government, there was also agreement that the characteristic domination of the economy by a "monopolistic clutch of corporations" should not be allowed. They argued, therefore, that economic development and job creation should aim at putting capital and "the ownership of production" in black hands. They advocated the development of the informal business sector and small industries in the black community as the most effective means of achieving these goals.

A few interviewees were more reserved in their views about the effectiveness of economic pressure used for political goals. This group argued that the unemployment resulting from economic upheaval would weaken the economic leverage that blacks have gained in recent years through job mobility and unionization.

Probably the most important, albeit disheartening, lessons that development planners have learned from experience with programs for alleviation of poverty and creation of employment are:

— Job creation per se is no guarantee of the alleviation of poverty; in many cases development programs have been accompanied by large increases in the number of working poor. Programs that create low-skill jobs often fail to provide a subsistence wage and thus, although they absorb a certain percentage of the unemployed, they contribute little to an improvement in living standards.
— While economic growth is a prerequisite for significant levels of job creation, it does not necessarily result in the creation of additional jobs. This is particularly true in South Africa, where the pattern of capital intensive investment has led to a consistent decline in the job creating capability of the modern sector economy despite high levels of economic growth.
— Better results have been achieved with policies designed to remove the factors constraining job creation than with those aimed at the introduction of entirely new development programs. In the case of South Africa this implies a reorientation from a capital intensive to a labor intensive pattern of economic development.
— If job creation is to be accompanied by a reduction in poverty, development efforts must specifically aim at the creation of jobs that can be filled by people from the poorest strata of the community, but which will, at the same time, pay a wage sufficient to provide for their basic needs.

Private or state sponsored employment creation programs need to take these observations into account if they hope to create opportunities for blacks to break out of the poverty cycle, rather than simply perpetuate dependence.

A number of black trade unions have begun to give attention to job creation schemes in light of the escalating retrenchment of black workers. Unionists interviewed suggested that such schemes might include training projects in skills such as brick laying, welding and plumbing that might contribute to community development. Little has been accomplished to date.

On the basis of existing patterns of economic development, economists estimate that by 2000 about 13 percent of the economically active African population will depend on the informal business sector for their income. However, between 40 and 50 percent will remain unemployed, and the job creation capacity of the modern sector economy, even at times of exceptional economic growth, is limited. Thus, for both economic and political reasons, the focus of any initiative aimed at alleviating black unemployment ought to be the expansion of the informal sector.

The informal business sector: Government and business leaders have cultivated the notion of "free enterprise" and small business development as a means of creating a black middle class as a bulwark against increasing black radicalism. Consequently, the concept of "free enterprise" is politically charged, and most blacks see small business development as a device to divide blacks further on the basis of class. Black attitudes are further clouded by the initiation of various programs by the government and the corporate sector aimed at the development of the informal business sector.

The Small Business Development Corporation was established with funds from the government and the private sector to provide loan capital and business expertise to small business enterprises. Interviewees were most critical of this organization both because of its close ties to government and because they believe that its lending criteria exclude most blacks. A number of major corporations — including Barlow Rand, Citibank and Mobil Oil — have recently initiated independent small business development programs.

The difficulty that many small black traders experience in supplying the necessary credit guarantees limits the number of blacks that benefit from these schemes. Interviewees emphasized that traditional business criteria could not be applied to black traders operating outside the formal business structure. Instead they advocated an approach that is "less concerned with spreading the gospel of free enterprise" and more concerned with increasing opportunities for subsistence.

The only black directed organization of this kind is the Get Ahead Foundation, whose board members include Soweto activist Nthatho Motlana and Desmond Tutu. The Get Ahead Foundation primarily provides low interest loans to small black enterprises such as sidewalk stalls, hawkers and home industries such as sewing groups and weavers. The Foundation also assists in the development of larger industries — such as brick making, textiles and publishing — providing management skills training and acting as a broker between black manufacturers and possible consumers.

URBAN HOUSING

The backlog of homes for Africans already settled in black townships adjacent to the white urban centers exceeds 500,000, and the demand for black urban housing is expected to average 200,000 per year between now and the turn of the century. Just to keep abreast of the new demand, the government would need to spend about $800 million annually for low income housing, and this does not take into consideration the backlog.

A major private sector organization, the Urban Foundation, was founded by leaders of the business community after the 1976 Soweto uprising to channel private sector funds into upgrading facilities in black townships. The Urban Foundation has concentrated on the provision of middle income housing in existing townships. Interviewees were vocal in their opinions about the Urban Foundation. Many argue that it is dedicated to the development of a black middle class as part of the strategy to pacify black opposition to apartheid, as reflected in the fact that many of the houses it provides are beyond the means of the average black person. Others suggest that it is simply "covering over the cracks of apartheid." However, some interviewees acknowledged that the Urban Foundation has an important role to play in the provision of housing and community facilities, and praised the Foundation's role in persuading government to allow blacks to own property and to change the influx control laws.

The Urban Foundation has increasingly concerned itself with the provision of low cost housing in squatter communities. This organization has been responsible for a large scale community development project in the Inanda squatter community in Natal and was to have begun the redevelopment of the Crossroads squatter camp outside Cape Town until the camp was destroyed in clashes among residents during May 1986.

There is enforced residential segregation in South Africa, and blacks may own homes and live only in black townships established on the periphery of white metropolitan areas. Most of these townships were originally established as labor camps, and many still lack infrastructure — paved roads, drainage, electricity or sewerage. All of those interviewed expressed deep resentment of residential segregation, but most acknowledged that the majority of blacks probably would have to continue to live in existing black townships after majority government because of the shortage of urban housing.

Thus the upgrading of infrastructure and community facilities was seen as an important priority. Several interviewees mentioned the Funda Center — a multi-purpose community center in Soweto — as a model for similar developments. Although the Funda Center was built by the Urban Foundation with financial support from a number of major South African and multinational corporations, it is now independently administered by a board composed of representatives of the different groups that use the center's facilities.

While upgrading infrastructure and community facilities is seen as important, the most pressing need, according to those interviewed, is to provide basic housing for the increasing number of migrants from the rural areas. Since the opportunities for subsistence in the rural areas are limited, many interviewees argued that urban migration should be encouraged as a way of alleviating the poverty cycle. However, the proponents of urban migration emphasized that basic housing and community facilities are an urgent priority if tension between settled communities and new arrivals is to be avoided.

The possibility of accelerated urban migration has been increased by the relaxation of the influx control laws for the 70 percent of blacks that do not reside in the four independent homelands. However, under strict prohibitions on squatting and trespassing legislated at the same time, blacks may effectively live in urban black townships only if they possess both a house and a job.

VICTIMS OF APARTHEID

Although programs aimed at assisting the victims of apartheid are more in line with humanitarian aid than with community development, interviewees emphasized the need to redress the immediate suffering of black people while trying to remedy the causes. As one interviewee put it, "Symbolism is important; helping victims of apartheid will establish whose side you're on."

Humanitarian assistance: Probably the best known program of this kind is the Black Sash — a group of white liberal women who since the 1950s have maintained offices in the main regions of the country to assist blacks with problems relating to housing, forced relocation, unemployment and other aspects of the law. Some blacks criticize these efforts for simply helping "the oppressed" cope with the status quo and not doing anything to change the law. Some question the political relevance of the organization because, as one interviewee put it, "They are rich whites trying to appease their consciences, by being nice to blacks." However, while most agree that the Black Sash is not in the vanguard of the liberation struggle, its commitment to assisting the victims of apartheid is unquestioned.

On a different level, humanitarian aid for blacks displaced by the escalating civil conflict or forced to relocate by the government is given priority. For example, in May 1986 more than 40,000 residents of the Crossroads squatter camp were displaced by the fighting that destroyed their makeshift homes. About 10,000 are still housed in tents supplied by the South African Red Cross and other relief agencies. World Vision — a California-based interdenominational Christian relief agency — provides meals for more than 2,500 refugees from the Crossroads camp every day.

The escalation of the internal conflict will undoubtedly lead to a greater need for "disaster relief" in the form of emergency housing, food and medical care. Until recently many urban blacks took refuge in the rural areas, but the conflict spread to these areas as well. Many blacks say the conflict in the rural areas is even more intense because the security forces and opposing black factions are less restrained by public attention and many atrocities go unreported. The "internal refugee" problem is expected to increase.

A number of community workers warned about the role of relief agencies in relieving the South African government of its moral obligation to provide adequate shelter and sustenance for displaced citizens — an argument that is particularly pertinent in view of the fact that most relief work is done among political refugees displaced by the deliberate actions and policies of the government. These interviewees argued that private relief agencies should place greater pressure on government to provide for the hungry and homeless victims of apartheid and that greater publicity should be given to the political causes of social dislocation.

Legal aid: The complexity of apartheid regulations implies that blacks are continuously coming up against the law. In recent years a network of privately funded and administered community advice centers has sprung up in townships around the country. The main function of the advice centers is to counsel community members on legal problems relating to a broad spectrum of day-to-day issues. These organizations are linked to a network of lawyers who volunteer their services as legal representatives. At the end of 1985, the Advice Centers Association (ACA) was formed to coordinate and facilitate the training of paralegal counselors, information and fundraising for all advice centers around the country. The ACA is closely linked to the Black Legal Education Center, founded in Johannesburg in 1984 by the Black Lawyers' Association (BLA) to provide a central training and legal referral center for the developing network of advice centers. The Legal Resources Center (LRC) — a white-run organization primarily committed to litigation on behalf of blacks in the higher courts — has established a considerable reputation for its innovative challenges to the interpretation of apartheid laws. In addition, the LRC is the principal legal counsel for the victims of apartheid laws, such as rural communities threatened with forced relocation and political detainees. In addition to offices in Johannesburg, Cape Town and Durban, a branch of the Legal Resources Center has recently been established in the impoverished and strife torn Eastern Cape with the aim of providing legal assistance to blacks living in that region. The Washington-based Southern Africa Legal Services and Education Project (Salslep) provides funds for legal assistance programs in Southern Africa and has supported the work of the LRC and BLA.

In another area, the Center for Applied Legal Studies (Cals), based at the University of the Witwatersrand, has had a major impact on the development of labor law since the legal recognition of black trade unions in 1979.

Interviewees emphasized the need to provide funding for the legal defense of political dissidents charged under South African security laws. The state has recently attempted to obstruct the activities of anti-apartheid groups by charging large numbers of their leaders with treason and engaging them in lengthy and costly trials. Furthermore, the families of political detainees suffer great economic hardship, and the need to provide humanitarian assistance to these families was stressed. The South African Council of Churches is a principal conduit for such funding.

In September 1986, the U.S. government provided $96,000 to finance legal action challenging various dimensions of the South African government's June 1986 emergency regulations, particularly the detention of children. This grant is administered by a Johannesburg-based association of white liberal lawyers known as Lawyers for Human Rights.

Victims of brutality: One of the most extreme aspects of black people's suffering under apartheid is police brutality. More than 2,000 blacks have been killed in political violence since August 1984, and scores more have been injured and brutalized in confrontations with the security forces. Often those who have been shot, beaten or raped by the security forces are afraid to present themselves to hospitals or clinics in the townships because police regularly arrest and imprison patients, citing their wounds as evidence of their roles in instigating violence.

Interviewees suggested the establishment of a trust fund — possibly under the auspices of the National Medical and Dental Association (NAMDA) — for the treatment of such victims at private clinics.

Many detainees suffer severe psychological trauma and physical abuse while in police detention. Between 8,000 and 12,000 political dissidents have been incarcerated since June 1986. The Detainees Parents Support Committee monitors the well-being of detainees and could be instrumental in administering funds for the treatment of detainees after release and the prosecution of security officials responsible for torturing and assaulting political prisoners.

REFUGEE PROGRAMS

Estimates of the number of black South African refugees in neighboring countries, Europe and the United States range from 200,000 to 500,000. There was some controversy among those interviewed about whether blacks in exile were more deserving of assistance than those remaining in the country. Most responded that those remaining in the country are bearing the brunt of apartheid and "that the real battle is being fought at home." However, many of the interviewees noted that almost everyone knows somebody who is in exile and that often refugees find conditions extremely harsh.

The best known refugee program is the Solomon Mahlangu Freedom College at Mazimbu in Tanzania. This school, run by the African National Congress, provides education for refugees and the children of refugees. The complex houses about 1,800 people and extends over 4,000 acres. In addition to preschool, primary and secondary school facilities, there is an agricultural training program and an adult education program. Several interviewees sounded a caveat about support for the Solomon Mahlangu Freedom College because they believed the school enrolls only the children of members of the ANC. Representatives of the ANC, when questioned, disputed this and said that perception is possibly the result of the fact that those refugees who find their way to Tanzania do so because they are ANC supporters.

Interviewees suggested that an extensive scholarship program to enable refugees to study at universities in other African countries would be a valuable contribution to refugee education. The bulk of scholarships available to South African refugees are administered by the United Nations Educational and Training Program for Southern Africa (UNETPSA). Several American agencies also administer scholarships for South African refugees, including the Bishop Desmond Tutu Southern Africa Refugee Scholarship Fund administered by the Phelps Stokes Fund in New York and the Southern African Training Program of the African-American Institute. In addition, the ANC has recently established the Freedom Charter Education Fund based in Washington, D.C., to channel private American funds into refugee education.

A number of those interviewed mentioned the fact that many refugees often had little to do and are "kicking their heels in a strange land." They advocated the initiation of programs in neighboring states for the training of refugees in skills that would be useful to South Africa after their return. Of particular value would be the training of refugees for posts in the civil service in majority governed South Africa. The precedent exists in the Namibia Institute in Lusaka, established by the United Nations to train "a government in exile" for Namibia.

DEVELOPING THE INSTITUTIONS OF A POST-APARTHEID SOCIETY

As indicated earlier, the focus of community development ought to be the creation of a firm social and political foundation for majority government in South Africa. The development of institutions that can contribute to the stability of a future government is as important as the alleviation of black social and economic disadvantage.

The alternative media: The general news media in South Africa are not only heavily restricted by the government, but with only one exception all major daily newspapers are controlled by one of four white-owned publishing houses. Interviewees argued that the "establishment media," as it is known, aims primarily at a white readership and, therefore, reflects a biased white interpretation of events. Furthermore, "to add insult to injury," as one interviewee put it, the major dailies publish separate "black editions" for their black readers.

In response to black disaffection with a white interpretation of the news, a number of independent, black run newspapers have emerged in recent years. These publications constitute what is called the "alternative media" and are mostly parochial news sheets published variously by trade unions, community groups and political organizations. The most significant of the alternative media publications is the *New Nation,* published by the Southern African Catholic Bishops' Conference and edited by former Nieman Fellow Zwelakhe Sisulu. First published in January 1986, the *New Nation* has quickly established a national readership and has been lauded for the quality of its journalism.

Other significant alternative media publications include *Grassroots,* published in Cape Town, and *Learn and Teach* magazine, published in Johannesburg. An organization for the promotion of the concept of an alternative media, known as Speak, operates in the Witwatersrand. Similarly, the Media and Resource Service (MARS) and the Interchurch Media Program, both based in Johannesburg, provide training in media skills and production facilities for community publications. In addition, an independent black publishing house, Skotaville Publishers, was established in 1981 for the publication of literary, academic and political works by black authors. Skotaville has published the writings of a number of prominent black political leaders, including Archbishop Desmond Tutu and Allan Boesak.

Interviewees emphasized the importance of the independent media in bridging the gulf between black and white society, but also in keeping the spirit of a free press alive in the face of severe restrictions. As one interviewee put it, "Even if the alternative media is not really any more free than the establishment media, its very existence is a symbol of faith, and must be kept alive." A number of interviewees pointed to the fact that an independent black press would have a vital role in ensuring an accurate record of events in the wake of a change in the distribution of political power in South Africa.

Leadership groups: The development of experienced and sophisticated leadership is obviously fundamental to the future of majority government. The principal training ground for black leadership is the large variety of organizations that represent different aspects of black society, including the black trade union movement, professional associations, the church, political organizations and smaller community groups.

A number of political activists and trade unionists argued that the effectiveness of "institutions of liberation" as one described them, such as the unions, progressive political groups and even the church, largely depends upon the promise of tangible improvements in the quality of life and the human dignity of ordinary people that can be held up as minor victories in the political struggle. A current example is the apparent inability of the National Education Crisis Committee (NECC) to persuade government to make concessions on black demands for change in the education system, compounded by its failure to make visible progress on the development of "people's education" because of state harassment and a lack of financial resources. Many interviewees pointed to the NECC as the last time that younger, more radical blacks would "acquiesce in the channels of moderation," as one interviewee aptly put it. Moreover, the failure of this coalition of parents, teachers and students to live up to expectations will intensify student disenchantment with the perceived passivity of their elders.

Increasingly, younger blacks are becoming disillusioned with, and disdainful of, non-violent channels of resistance and established leadership. Many interviewees spoke of near anarchy in black society that has left established black leaders without influence. Some voiced their concern that a majority government might be destabilized by the increasingly radical expectations of younger blacks so that, in the words of one interviewee, "Our finest hour might turn into the darkest in our history." Thus, interviewees emphasized the need to strengthen institutions that could harness the leadership skills of younger blacks and provide the organizational base essential for the maintenance of a semblance of order.

Prime among these organizations is the black labor movement. Unionists interviewed by IRRC confirmed that there is strong suspicion among black labor leaders that the AFL-CIO and the African American Labor Center (AALC) of the AFL-CIO is manipulated by the CIA and that many unions would not accept funding from this organization. Most black unions, however, will accept funding only from international labor federations and sister unions. There are also a number of training and technical support organizations that receive funding from other sources and that make an important contribution to the emergent labor movement. Particularly significant are the Johannesburg-based Technical Advice Group (TAG), which is concerned principally with occupational health and safety issues; the Industrial Aid Society, a workers' advice service; and the Urban Training Project, a multi-purpose union training center. Moreover, black unions are increasingly making use of the newly created Independent Mediation Services of South Africa (IMSSA) to mediate in labor-management disputes rather than the cumbersome and often controversial industrial court. Union leaders ascribed the increasing reliance on independent mediation to the perceived anti-worker bias of the industrial court.

Whereas national union federations provide political leadership for the black South African labor movement as a whole, the local union leadership is vital in representing workers and in providing linkage with the broader black community. Similarly, interviewees identified the network of civic associations as critically important in mobilizing and representing the interests of local communities. In addition, professional associations such as the Black Lawyers' Association, the Black Management Forum and the Media Workers Association were identified as representing important interests.

The labor movement and the civic associations regularly organize leadership training courses for their own members. In addition, a number of institutions run programs for the training of black leadership, including the Community Resource and Information Center (CRIC), the United States-South Africa Leader Exchange Program (Ussalep), Sached and the Wilgespruit Fellowship Center — a multi-purpose training facility outside Johannesburg.

Interviewees emphasized that leadership training has to be done "on the job" because black leaders could not be taken out of circulation for any length of time. This implies that black leadership training ought to be more informal and concentrate on the specific needs of the particular leaders involved.

ORGANIZATIONAL NETWORK

Few black community development organizations have a national network. Moreover, there is little cooperation among various organizations with similar interests. Some of the reasons are fierce competition for financial resources, differing ideological and political perceptions, and the generally personalized nature of organizational leadership. Many community development projects evolve from the initiative of one person or a small group of dynamic individuals. The initiators often jealously guard their programs from political rivals, with the result that personality clashes at the leadership level are common.

The proliferation of black community organizations in recent years has given rise to the idea of a coordinating mechanism. Black organizations fiercely resist formal coordination, particularly of funds, because, as one interviewee put it, "No institution is above politics." Any such coordinating group would have great difficulty maintaining political credibility because "those that bore a grudge against the way it dispensed funds would go out of their way to discredit it." Another interviewee added that "political neutrality is impossible, one can at best try for a balance, but in South Africa what is balanced to one person is biased to another."

Most black community groups have little more than a basic administrative structure or capability, and it is often necessary for donors to channel resources to smaller community projects through administratively more sophisticated intermediary organizations. An effective intermediary organization is the Trust for Christian Outreach and Education, which acts as the administrative umbrella for a host of small community projects in different parts of the country. The Trust is not only the conduit for financial resources, but also assists smaller groups develop administrative competence.

The role of an intermediary organization is not a substitute for developing administrative and organizational skills in grassroots organizations. A key priority is the development of an institutional network capable of absorbing increasing financial and other resources. However, most community workers argue against the development of a few large institutions. They maintain that the bigger the organization and the more funding it receives from abroad, the more likely it is to attract the unfavorable attention of the South African government. Black community organizations are regular targets for harassment by state authorities, ranging from the destruction of assets to the confiscation of records and the detention of personnel. A network of smaller, low profile community groups is far less vulnerable. Furthermore, the regular imprisonment of prominent black leaders underscores the imperative of developing a large cadre of skilled community leaders that are able to fill the breach.

Among the nationally based organizations that can facilitate access to smaller regional networks and local groups are the church, political organizations and trade unions.

The church: One of the difficulties of working through national anti-apartheid organizations is that they are liable to regular persecution that affects their ability to operate freely and effectively. Probably the single national organization that enjoys some immunity from state repression is the church. The church is often the pivot of local organization and therefore is well placed to facilitate access to local groups and individuals.

The South African Council of Churches is the largest federation of English-speaking Protestant churches, and it has regional branches throughout the country. The Southern African Catholic Bishops' Conference, based in Pretoria, also maintains offices in the major centers, which in turn are connected to local parishes. Moreover, there are a number of interdenominational organizations that have strong community links in the different regions — particularly Diakonia in Natal and the Interdenominational African Ministers' Association of South Africa (Idamasa) in the Eastern Cape.

The church has been seeking new relevance in the black struggle and has increasingly come to play the role of mediator and community activist, responding to the demands of a younger and more radical generation. The most sensible point of embarkation in seeking access to local groups thus is the regional office of the church organization concerned.

Political organizations: One of the disadvantages of working through either of the principal anti-apartheid organizations — Azapo or the UDF — is the partisan label this might place on an initiative, which would complicate contact with other groups. Moreover, these organizations are under constant threat of persecution and their operations are often hindered, as reflected by the government's October 1986 imposition of a prohibition on the UDF's receipt of foreign funds. Furthermore, the effectiveness of a regional office depends on the strength of leadership in that particular region and thus organizational reliability is varied.

Whereas the guidance of the national leaders of these groups is most important, they are less effective in lending practical assistance in the implementation and development of particular local community projects. Regional groups, some of which undertake very useful community project work, are members or affiliates of either Azapo or the UDF, but often the link is informal. Nonetheless, the endorsement of national leaders will certainly facilitate local access.

Trade unions: The black labor federations (Cosatu, Cusa and Azactu) have an extensive national organizational network, but for the most part the unions are hard pressed to keep up with their own work. Nevertheless, the unions and their regional branches are well placed to facilitate initial access to local community leadership. There is a lot of overlap among union leaders and local community organizations. In the major centers the support of the principal unions in the region would be of immeasurable value in securing political credibility and in mobilizing community support.

Other associations: A variety of professional and special interest groups maintain a national organizational network and thus are well placed to act as intermediaries for administratively less sophisticated community groups. Examples include the South African Black Social Workers' Association (Sabswa), the National African Federated Chamber of Commerce (Nafcoc), the Black Lawyers' Association, the African Teachers' Association of South Africa (Atasa), the Health Workers' Association and the National Medical and Dental Association.

It is essential, however, that the grassroots recipient agree to having one of these intermediary organizations act as an administrative go-between. Moreover, every effort should be made to ensure that the administrative capabilities of the intended recipient are upgraded as quickly as possible.

REGIONAL CONSIDERATIONS

The country is generally broken into five principal regions — the Witwatersrand, the Western Cape, the Eastern Cape, the Orange Free State, and Natal — and circumstances and conditions vary considerably among the various regions. Although the level of black impoverishment is so high that it is difficult to talk of some areas being more deprived than others, poverty is undoubtedly more severe in some regions. The Free State and the Eastern Cape are areas where conditions for blacks are particularly harsh. There is little industry in either of these regions, and thus black employment is mostly in agriculture, where workers are among the most poorly paid. Moreover, facilities and infrastructure in the black townships abutting the smaller towns of the Eastern Cape and Free State are particularly rudimentary, and many of these towns have become centers of local resistance as a result.

Interviewees were critical of the almost exclusive community development focus on the major metropolitan centers, and they accuse donors of doing what is easiest and not what is most necessary. One interviewee explained that donors "prefer to deal with those that already have a head start" because "getting off the beaten track is more uncertain." Blacks accuse donors of using their projects to seek publicity and maintain that the publicity value is reduced if the projects are not located in major centers. Also, many blacks believe that corporate donors in particular are concerned only about those areas where their black work force lives, so that "corporate responsibility really takes on the form of extended worker benefits."

RELIABLE MANAGEMENT

Although choosing organizations with the appropriate political credentials is most important, this factor should not obscure the need to ensure appropriate organizational management and accounting skills. Different criteria might be applied to various organizations, depending on their sophistication, but a general evaluation could include the following:

— does the organization have an unauditied or audited financial statement?
— does the organization have any full-time administrative employees, and what are their qualifications?
— are the trustees of the organization reliable and politically credible public figures?
— what is the organization's track record?
— what other sources of financial support does the organization have?

There are two possible approaches to community development — each with different implications for the nature of involvement and the commitment of resources. The first might be called the "ad hoc" approach and the second the "developmental approach."

The ad hoc approach assumes that the objective is to provide financial support without getting embroiled in the day-to-day administration of the project. It also implies a more specific and less broadly based conception of community development needs.

This implies a more distant, anonymous attitude where programs for support are selected on merit according to set criteria such as administrative sophistication, quality of leadership and practicality of objectives. This is the conventional approach adopted by donors. The developmental approach, on the other hand, implies a direct involvement in the planning and development of community development initiatives. This role is more akin to that of a development agency and offers the donor the advantage of direct involvement in shaping the project and monitoring progress.

Although interviewees viewed the developmental approach, in terms of commitment and objectives, as preferable, they considered it important that black-run organizations be given the responsibility of developing and administering community development proposals. Interviewees complained that donors too often choose to work through well established organizations rather than risk supporting newer community groups because they suspect that black community groups do not have the administrative capability. Many interviewees suggested that an integral part of any community development initiative ought to be the training of blacks to manage and develop the undertaking. A number pointed out that the training of blacks in administrative and organizational skills is in itself an important contribution to the development of community leadership.

Most black community development groups are organized around a dominant personality or a small number of like minded individuals. Although some groups have a large number of members on paper, often the role of the broader membership is rather informal. With few exceptions, such organizations lead a hand-to-mouth existence struggling to raise funds to cover basic administrative overheads and to maintain project work. Few are sufficiently well funded to afford full time personnel, and most often work is done voluntarily by individuals who have full time jobs of their own. As a result, many smaller community organizations find it difficult to raise money because they do not have the sophisticated administrative capability of more established groups.

One black community leader said that "donors are seldom prepared to break new ground, but it is the first furrow which is most difficult to plough." In other words, the initial training and support that an organization receives is crucial in encouraging support from more skeptical donors. One way of broadening an organization's financial support base is to encourage it to find matching funding from other sources.

Although from the recipient's point of view it is helpful to be able to plan on long term funding, the changing political situation makes it advisable for donors to retain the right to review commitments annually. It is necessary to monitor and evaluate both the political context of a particular project and its programmatic merits continuously, and to retain sufficient flexibility to withdraw support from projects that no longer meet the original criteria.

WHAT RESOURCES ARE MOST NEEDED?

In keeping with the emphasis on a developmental approach, most interviewees argued that a combination of resources — money, technical skills and equipment — are most needed. It was argued that it is difficult to establish a categoric set of priorities because needs differ acccording to circumstances. Financial assistance is obviously basic to any undertaking, but most of those interviewed emphasized the need for skills training to enable blacks to develop and manage community development initiatives. As mentioned earlier, community development is seen as a process of "empowerment" through which blacks acquire the skills of self-reliance. Training in administrative and organizational skills is fundamental to this process.

One interviewee said that "blacks need to develop confidence in themselves," and he advocated that donor agencies cultivate a "partnership" with appropriate black community development organizations. The partnership should not be based simply on "financial handouts," but on "nurturing the necessary skills" and "channeling resources" for the sustained development of the particular undertaking. A number of other interviewees emphasized that blacks resent the perpetuation of dependency through what one called "the big handout."

What another interviewee described as "checkbook philanthropy" was generally scorned as lacking in any purpose other than the gratification of the donor. Many of the interviewees echoed the opinion that blacks do not want to appear ungrateful, but as one put it, "The problem cannot be solved simply by throwing money at it."

III.
AMERICAN INVOLVEMENT IN COMMUNITY DEVELOPMENT IN SOUTH AFRICA

Growing American involvement in community development programs in South Africa and the promise of even greater involvement has increased the concern of black South Africans that much of the assistance is misdirected. A belief prevails that the focus of American assistance is biased toward support for initiatives that most closely conform to U.S. political and social preconceptions. As a result, the focus of many American-supported initiatives conflicts with the goals of credible, black anti-apartheid organizations. This fact, in turn, makes it difficult for such organizations to be unequivocally associated with American institutions.

In addition, attitudes toward American philanthropy in South Africa have become intertwined with black antipathy toward the U.S. administration's policy of "constructive engagement," and with demands by many black South Africans that multinational corporations pull out of South Africa. This raises the questions of whether continued U.S. involvement is possible, and of how American organizations might improve their political standing with black South Africans.

BLACK ATTITUDES TO AMERICAN INVOLVEMENT

Interviews with black South Africans about American involvement in community development elicited strong emotions. All of those interviewed attested to the fact that most black South Africans feel a strong antipathy toward the United States based on several factors — an ideological aversion to capitalism and perceived American imperialism, the conviction that the Reagan administration is supporting the apartheid regime, and the feeling that American companies, by refusing to withdraw, support the administration's policy of constructive engagement. Interviewees noted that at the intellectual level distinction is drawn between government officials and other Americans, but in general everything American is painted with the same brush. As one interviewee put it, "In the minds of the masses the United States is firmly established as an enemy of the people."

Constructive engagement: Constructive engagement is the term adopted by the Reagan administration to characterize its policy of encouraging political reform in South Africa through a process of "quiet diplomacy" with South Africa's white minority rulers. Black South Africans revile this notion because, they argue, Pretoria has taken strength from the sympathetic approach of the Reagan administration. Thus constructive engagement is construed as contributing to the perpetuation of apartheid.

Interviewees maintained that constructive engagement is premised on the appeasement of whites and completely ignores the attitudes and aspirations of blacks. One interviewee said that, in the eyes of blacks, "Reagan's policy [on South Africa] puts Americans in the same camp as the white oppressors."

Black antipathy to constructive engagement is underscored by a general aversion to what many blacks see as international American imperialism. Recent rallying points for black opposition to U.S. imperialism are the U.S. support for anti-government forces in Nicaragua, the bombing of Libya and the approval of a U.S. aid package to Unita — the anti-communist resistance movement in Angola. In March 1986, the U.S. State Department announced that the United States would supply weapons to Unita, including the controversial Stinger anti-aircraft missile. Unita receives large scale assistance from the South African government, and American support for what is seen as the subversion of an independent African government is particularly abhorrent to black South Africans.

Black reaction to the congressional override of President Reagan's veto of a comprehensive package of economic sanctions against South Africa in September 1986 was muted. A number of leading blacks approached for their reaction shrugged it off as long overdue. Although all applauded Congress for its challenge to the policy of constructive engagement, a number expressed skepticism about the extent to which the legislation would actually effect a policy change toward South Africa. One interviewee said that the sanctions bill would certainly "go some of the way in redeeming the United States" in the eyes of black South Africans, but that blacks generally had difficulty "separating the imposition of sanctions against South Africa from American aid to Unita." It is clear that black attitudes toward the United States are not simply a function of American policy toward South Africa, but are influenced by perceptions of American global policy.

Most interviewees were of the opinion that the difference between Democrats and Republicans is principally rhetorical. Some referred to the Carter administration as having the right rhetoric on South Africa, but even less impact on apartheid than the current administration. One community leader described Americans as having "semantic differences about domestic policies, but when it comes to challenging U.S. foreign policy they rally around the flag." Consequently a number of interviewees said they had a policy of deliberate avoidance of American officials and noted extreme sensitivity among many black organizations to accepting funds linked to the U.S. government. Most interviewees agreed that passage of the sanctions bill probably would not affect this position.

Disinvestment: Mention has already been made of the fact that, with the exception of the Inkatha movement, all major black political organizations, the black labor movement, the South African Council of Churches and the Catholic Bishops' Conference support disinvestment. Interviewees explained that black South Africans do not need to debate whether foreign companies should withdraw because most blacks accept withdrawal as a step in accelerating the demise of apartheid. They explained that the withdrawal of foreign companies and the divestment of stock in companies doing business in South Africa were originally conceived as elements in the strategy of black resistance to galvanize international pressure against the Pretoria government. Therefore, they argue, disinvestment is not an issue for black South Africans. As one put it, "It is something Americans must make up their minds about." However, opinion surveys conducted during 1985 and 1986 by the Center for Applied Social Sciences, the Human Sciences Research Council, the *London Sunday Times* and the Community Agency for Social Enquiry indicate that a core of only about 25 percent of blacks support withdrawal unconditionally.

Interviewees expressed the belief that U.S. companies have been the main focus of the push for disinvestment because they have taken a higher public profile than most foreign companies through the Sullivan code of employment practices and activities in the area of social responsibility. Blacks, therefore, have felt challenged to formulate a political response to these programs. Furthermore, some noted that American business in South Africa is lumped in the same bracket as constructive engagement. Indeed, a number of interviewees said that in the minds of "the masses" American investment in South Africa only began with the election of President Reagan. More radical blacks describe American companies as the "missionaries of international capitalism" and suggest that U.S. business is more zealous in its propagation of the capitalist ethic than most others.

When questioned about the implications of disinvestment most interviewees acknowledged that foreign investment would be needed if the economic development of South Africa is to be sustained after the advent of majority government. However, they said that a black government would be selective about those foreign investors permitted to do business in the country. Specifically it was suggested that companies that do not withdraw now will not be welcomed back. Moreover, they said the emotional antipathy of the mass of less well informed blacks toward American business would make it difficult for a majority government to give U.S. companies unrestricted access to South Africa in the future.

Yet there is a curious contradiction between the forceful and unanimous calls for disinvestment on the one hand, and the equally forceful plea for American resources for community development on the other. Interviewees explained that disinvestment is intended as a political action, but blacks have never thought of disinvestment as absolving Americans of further involvement in South Africa. Blacks do not want to be abandoned to their fate, either now or after majority government. One interviewee said "blacks must be allowed their moments of protest" so that "when they put on their political hats they can bite the hand that feeds them."

Others elaborated on this point by saying that blacks are aware of their dependence on American resources and despise their dependency because it makes a mockery of political ideals. They noted that this is a general Third World phenomenon. One interviewee observed that in a situation of political uncertainty and insecurity "it is often difficult to distinguish between ally and foe, everything is viewed with suspicion and attack is wiser than defense."

Most interviewees were emphatic that American investment in community development must not be seen as an alternative to the withdrawal of U.S. companies. They noted that a number of American organizations have propagated the notion of greater social investment to counter the black demand for disinvestment. All agreed that this was counterproductive because it diluted the black perception of the humane commitment of American agencies and underscored the generally held belief that Americans "are just here for the profits," as one interviewee put it.

American social and political preconceptions: Almost without exception, interviewees expressed the opinion that Americans "don't listen." One put it most aptly, "Americans sieve everything they hear through a deeply ingrained set of values — discarding anything that does not strike a familiar or comfortable chord."

The American world view is premised upon the values of capitalist free enterprise and democracy. One interviewee remarked, "Americans are so secure in these values as the mainstay of the American dream that they cannot conceive of other people not having the same ideals." Yet another said that Americans have an innate conviction that the values on which the United States is founded are supremely superior and that the rest of the world should be "converted to the American way of thinking." Generally interviewees expressed irritation about the superficial nature of American concern and the characteristic assumption by Americans that "they have all the answers."

One interviewee succinctly echoed the views of a number of others. He said, "Americans are pushy about being exonerated for constructive engagement and yet they always put their feet in their mouths because basically they cannot fake an understanding of the black struggle." He continued, "If only Americans would stop believing that they can empathize with the struggle in this country, they would realize that this is not an outpost of American slavery waiting for the civil rights movement to catch up with it."

Interviewees argued that parallels between the American civil rights movement and the liberation struggle in South African are misleading. Unlike the United States, they note, blacks in South Africa outnumber whites seven to one. Moreover, there is no bill of rights that can be invoked by blacks who are victims of discrimination, and blacks in South Africa do not even have a rhetorically sympathetic government to which they can appeal for equal treatment under the law. More generally interviewees said that Americans assume a patronizing attitude by suggesting that they empathize with the struggle of black South Africans. As one put it, "Nobody can tell me where it aches."

Most interviewees expressed the opinion that American involvement in community development is motivated more by political goals than by humanitarian concerns. The suspicion that the CIA operates through some of the most reputable American philanthropic foundations was often voiced. Some interviewees said that this concern ought to preclude any dealings by anti-apartheid organizations with American agencies; others were of the opinion that since all money is politically tainted it is acceptable to take it from American donor agencies as well. Most agreed that the key issue is whether the recipient organization believes it is being politically manipulated by the donor.

A number of those interviewed suggested that blacks suspect Americans are trying to choose the government they would like to see in South Africa. One interviewee said that "American agencies are predetermining the political relevance of particular individuals and organizations according to American interests." Other interviewees said they suspected that American organizations hope the United Democratic Front will grow to overshadow the seemingly more extreme African National Congress. Thus they believe Americans concentrate their support mostly on the less radical, non-racial organizations. (Chief Gatsha Buthelezi, on the other hand, said in a speech in September 1986 that U.S. government funds are being put in the hands of extremists.) Yet another interviewee said the United States "is buying a strategic presence in South Africa," but he noted, "because blacks accept American money does not mean they will support American politics."

Government funding: Compared with aid to other African countries, U.S. government development aid to South Africa is small. In 1986 the Agency for International Development (AID) budgeted just over $20 million for programs in South Africa. The bulk of this money is spent on scholarships for between 80 and 100 black South Africans to study at American universities each year, and on an internal scholarship fund that will provide financial assistance to about 800 black students at South African universities over the next five years. The remainder is spent on such areas as emergency relief for the victims of apartheid, grants to human rights organizations and self-help development projects, training for black unionists and grassroots leadership development programs. No funding is channeled through agencies of the South African government.

Interviewees were divided on this funding. Some argued that acceptance of this money would imply endorsement by black South Africans of the Reagan administration's policies. Proponents of this argument see this type of American aid as a direct attempt at political manipulation. They noted that the depth of anti-American feeling among blacks generally makes it very difficult for any organization that wishes to retain credibility with black South Africans to accept American government money. On the other hand, some argued that many credible black South African organizations do accept American government funding, and that the key issue is a matter of whether the recipient has complete control of the funds. This group asserted that all funds are acceptable as long as there are "no strings attached." In other words, black organizations must be free to pursue their own goals without undue interference from donors. This is an extension of the notion that "all money is tainted" alluded to earlier, but as one black community leader put it, "when it passes through my hands it is washed clean." Other interviewees reacted to this telling statement by saying that while some black leaders who have large reserves of credibility could afford to adopt this attitude, most leaders are under constant scrutiny by younger activists and, in the words of one, "When the time comes, they will find whatever evidence they can lay their hands on — accepting money from Reagan is enough to let me burn."

The Sullivan signatories: In 1977 a core group of the major American corporations doing business in South Africa committed themselves to a set of employment principles devised by the Rev. Leon Sullivan — a Baptist minister, longtime civil rights campaigner and member of the General Motors board of directors. The original purpose of the Sullivan principles was ending racial discrimination on the shop floor and desegregating the facilities of U.S. businesses in South Africa. The principles were expanded in 1984 to include community development initiatives and lobbying the South African government for political reform.

The number of American companies participating in the Sullivan program — which includes a rigorous reporting and monitoring procedure — exceeded 170 of a total of 257 U.S. companies in South Africa in August 1986. Between 1977 and 1985 corporate signatories to the Sullivan principles spent a total of $158 million on Sullivan-related programs, about half on community development and half on workplace reforms. This figure is expected to exceed $200 million by the the end of 1986.

Blacks are generally critical of the Sullivan effort. Some argue that it is an attempt to deflect pressure for disinvestment, but the most fundamental criticism voiced by interviewees was that the Sullivan principles were orginally devised without consultation with or participation by black South Africans and that this attitude continues to characterize the way in which the principles are implemented. One interviewee said, "Blacks find it hard to applaud a point scoring system devised and monitored in Philadelphia, because they are not part of it."

Furthermore, interviewees criticized the Sullivan principles for being an essentially ameliorative effort that has not contributed to any fundamental change in the apartheid system. A number of interviewees said that Sullivan signatories are quick to point out how much they have spent, but as one put it, "When you sit back, what has been accomplished with all this money?" They made the argument that the Sullivan signatories are too concerned with "winning brownie points for their company" and thus the impact has been dissipated in a host of diverse activities that have had no cumulative effect on the alleviation of black poverty or the dismantling of apartheid. Most interviewees readily acknowledged that employees of American companies are probably better off than counterparts at other companies and that individuals who have directly benefited from Sullivan programs would see it as a useful initiative. But, they argued, "Making apartheid easier for some does not change it for anybody."

Although some interviewees agreed that blacks generally overestimate the influence of American companies on the South African government, most said they thought American companies had engaged in a great deal of window dressing. Said one employee of an American company, "They [Sullivan signatories] have spent years evading the political question — just look how few black managers there are in American companies — so as not to offend the bulk of their white employees." The small number of black managers has political connotations for blacks, in that they argue that whites do not want to relinquish control to blacks. A number of interviewees noted that even the desegregation of workplace facilities is a facade. Said another American company employee, "There are no more signs in the toilets and in the cafeteria, but we know our place."

Yet another interviewee underscored this point by noting that "the corporate culture in American companies is for the best part just a microcosm of racial discrimination in the rest of South Africa." Others said that American companies had implemented apartheid laws in their businesses, such as the pass laws, in the same way as other companies and pointed out that they paid taxes to the South African government. They argued that American firms would win respect from blacks if they were more consistent in their defiance of government. Examples of such defiance include housing black employees in white areas, protecting employees from prosecution for anti-apartheid activities and withholding taxes. But they argued that it is U.S. corporate reticence about civil disobedience that lumps them, in the perception of blacks, with supporters of apartheid.

Interviewees asserted that American companies had invited public scrutiny by adopting a political profile and that if they are genuine in their commitment to changing their corporate ethos they would heed black criticism. But most said they saw no evidence of willingness to do this. They argued that few American companies in South Africa have black directors on their local boards and that consultation with blacks is generally limited to those few black managers employed by U.S. companies. Some interviewees noted that these individuals are inhibited in how directly they criticize their own bosses.

Interviewees proposed that American companies form consultative committees made up of credible community leaders, unionists and church leaders to direct the community development initiatives of Sullivan signatories. Supporters of this idea argue that the Sullivan program will be suspect until it is demonstrably directed by blacks. One interviewee summed it up succinctly: "Until blacks are accomplices in the process, they will be the accusers."

Administration of the Sullivan program in South Africa was restructured in early 1986 to allow for greater participation by blacks. The coordinator of the Signatory Association, as it is known, told IRRC that "although there have been significant improvements, a lot will have to be done to change black perceptions of the inadequacy of the program." This may not occur. In May 1985, Rev. Sullivan announced that if "apartheid has not, in fact, ended legally and actually as a system within the next 24 months" he would call for the complete withdrawal of all American firms from South Africa. The lack of progress in ending apartheid, coupled with the accelerated withdrawal of American companies from South Africa, have placed the future of the Sullivan program in jeopardy. There is uncertainty whether American companies remaining in South Africa after May 1987 will sustain the Sullivan initiative.

Major U.S. initiatives: A number of the larger American corporations in South Africa have recently made significant financial commitments to black community development. In 1984, IBM announced that it would spend $15 million on education, small business development and rural development projects over the next five years. This was followed shortly by announcements from Firestone and Honeywell that they too would commit substantial funds to educational projects — particularly the development of Khanya College. Early in 1986, Coca-Cola announced the creation of "equal opportunity funds" to be administered by a group of mostly black South African trustees — including Archbishop Desmond Tutu and the Rev. Allan Boesak — for education and community development — with an initial grant of $10 million. Mobil Oil, in turn, has created the Mobil Foundation in South Africa, which will make grants worth $20 million over five years. Funds from this foundation will be allocated to three priority areas — education, black business development and rural development programs.

Both IBM and Coca-Cola have subsequently announced the sale of their business assets in South Africa. However, spokesmen for both companies assured IRRC that withdrawal from South Africa would not affect existing community development commitments.

A number of the leading American philanthropies have committed money over the years to black development projects. In 1985, The Ford Foundation spent $2.5 million, Carnegie Corporation $738,000 and The Rockefeller Foundation $500,000. The bulk of this funding has supported black educational organizations, legal assistance groups and training programs for black leaders. In addition, a number of international relief agencies, such as World Vision and the International Red Cross, have maintained humanitarian and relief operations in South Africa. In October 1986 the South African goverment ordered International Red Cross workers out of South Africa in retaliation for the suspension of South African government representation to the International Red Cross Conference in Geneva. The work of the South African Red Cross is not directly affected by this move.

Interviewees made a distinction between what they called the "business foundations" and philanthropic institutions. There was consensus that blacks view the former with a great deal of cynicism, because they are perceived as efforts on the part of business to appease opponents of the American corporate presence in South Africa. Nonetheless, most interviewees acknowledged that blacks would vie for funding from the "business foundations" because the need for funding is so great. However, as one community leader put it, "Even though people are hungry, they don't go there with their whole hearts." Others were at pains to point out that black acceptance of funding from the "business foundations" should not be construed as support for American business in South Africa. They noted that the political support of blacks cannot be bought, and many of them dismissed the exercise as costly public relations. One summed up this view in terms of "a splurge of corporate largesse that will be mopped up, but won't buy American companies any political leeway with blacks."

When questioned about the endorsement of some of these "business foundations" by prominent black political figures, interviewees were derisive of the significance that Americans attach to this. Most responded that Americans imagine that Allan Boesak and Desmond Tutu are the only black leaders of consequence because they are well known in the United States. In their view, while Boesak and Tutu are respected figures, the real leadership is much closer to the grassroots. One added, "Tutu and Boesak are there to appease the American constituency, but fancy letterheads don't impress blacks."

What one interviewee called the "traditional American foundations" — referring to Ford, Carnegie and Rockefeller — were praised for their contribution to the development of anti-apartheid institutions in South Africa. Interviewees noted that most significant community development undertakings in South Africa received funding from at least one of these institutions at some time in their history. The role of these organizations in advancing "seed money" for new initiatives was particularly lauded because this has provided the base from which greater financial support could be mustered. In this way the "traditional foundations" have contributed significantly to the development of black institutions.

However, black consciousness loyalists were critical of the perceived inclination of these institutions toward non-racial and less radical groups. They argued that the "traditional foundations" support favored leaders and organizations, and give them relevance that they might not deserve. Some thought they are engaged in deliberate efforts to influence the political complexion of a majority government, while others said that they would have only as much political influence as blacks allowed. This group argued that blacks would not tolerate any grantmaking relationship that seemed to impose political conditions on the recipient.

A number of interviewees echoed the view that the "traditional foundations" have a political agenda, but there were different opinions on the influence of political values on grantmaking. Some argued that all grantmaking is inevitably subjective, while others thought that the "traditional foundations" were least likely to be influenced by politics, because, as one interviewee put it, "these are the professionals."

Educational institutions: More than 100 American colleges and universities now have black South African students in attendance. The bulk of these students are sponsored by the South African Education Program discussed in Chapter II. In addition, a number of educational institutions have raised money from students, trustees and faculty for scholarships for blacks to attend universities in South Africa or have specifically earmarked funds to bring additional black students to the United States.

However, some institutions have burned their fingers by launching intern programs for their students in South Africa, or providing scholarships for black South Africans to attend integrated universities in South Africa, without adequate consultation with either their student bodies or black South African leaders. A recent example is the shelving of the planned $1 million Harvard-South Africa intern program. Although the initiative seems to have been plagued by a variety of problems, the issue that rendered it unworkable was failure to consult in advance with appropriate black South Africans and the anti-apartheid activists in the Harvard student body. A no less controversial example is the New England Board of Higher Education's South Africa scholarship fund, which has raised $230,000 for 31 black students to attend "open universities" in South Africa. Student activists both in the United States and in South Africa have criticized this and similar programs for putting money into the hands of "government-controlled" universities, rather than progressive organizations independent of the state.

A number of universities have offered visiting teaching posts for black South African academics or have initiated a variety of educational support programs in South Africa. Shaw University, for example, plans to maintain a coordinating office in South Africa to channel U.S. educational resources to black South African teachers. Boston University has designed a program to improve the writing skills of black South African journalists, and Indiana University is a major participant in the development of Khanya College. In addition, Georgetown University has recently announced that it will provide advanced training in the United States for black South African lawyers.

These well-intentioned initiatives are not without controversy in South Africa. The first issue of dispute among black interviewees was the notion that direct involvement by American educational institutions is a breach of the international cultural and academic boycott of South Africa. A number felt strongly that a line had to be drawn between scholarships for black South African students and the actual participation of U.S. academics or teaching interns in government sponsored educational institutions. Most felt that if visiting American academics and teachers were placed in black schools and universities they would lend credibility to the status quo in black education and contribute little to changing the system. Participation by Americans in non-government programs is less controversial, but there was agreement that such participation should be only at the request of credible black organizations. On the other hand, all felt that scholarships that assist blacks in furthering their education are a positive contribution to black advancement. However, as discussed in Chapter II, there are differences of opinion about the relative merits of overseas and local study.

A further factor contributing to the controversy surrounding the interest of U.S. educational institutions in South Africa is the notion that many have initiated scholarship and other programs either as an alternative to complete divestment from companies doing busines in South Africa, or in an attempt to pacify anti-apartheid activists on their campuses. Most interviewees felt that these motives are unacceptable and that black South Africans should decline scholarships from American schools where this is the case.

Further controversy surrounds the way in which students are selected for scholarships. Without exception, those interviewed expressed the opinion that credible black South Africans should be responsible for the selection of candidates for scholarships. Most stressed the importance of political impartiality in the selection of students. Some expressed the opinion that the existing selection procedures are biased against students with black consciousness inclinations. As indicated earlier, there is no clear evidence of discrimination against candidates on the basis of political conviction. The key issue seems to be ensuring that the selection committee is representative of all major political groups.

At least some of the criticism of U.S. scholarship programs appears to spring from political pressure from South African exiles. Interviewees explained that black South African students in the United States are under pressure from South African political exiles, their American peers and activists in South Africa to take a radical stand. As a result, many find it expedient to criticize the scholarship programs. Most interviewees made the point that exiles in the United States should be given equal consideration for scholarships, but the notion that "exiles are more deserving than others" is unacceptable.

GUIDELINES FOR AMERICAN INVOLVEMENT

Interviewees attested to the fact that the antipathy of most black South Africans toward the United States is based as much on their perception of a characteristic American brusqueness and arrogance as any ideological aversion. Indeed, a number of interviewees pointed out that blacks do not have the same qualms about Europeans, with whom there are often ideological differences too. One interviewee offered his impression that "Americans do not have the time to find out what is really going on, they only come here so they can say they have seen the suffering." Yet another said, "Americans have the arrogance of a superpower and so anything that seems to challenge the supposed superiority of the American way of thinking is seen by Americans as an ideological affront, and the challenger as an enemy." He added, "Americans always end up defending their own beliefs, rather than trying to appreciate the reasons why others might think differently."

Despite strong criticism of American attitudes and an underlying political suspicion of the United States on the part of black South Africans, no one suggested that American support for community development is not needed or should not be increased. On the contrary, interviewees pointed to the enormity of South Africa's development needs. Most spoke in terms of the needs of majority government to secure political stability, but others spoke only in humanitarian terms. Both groups argued that the perception of South Africa as highly developed is false and that the development of human resources is imperative if the country is to live up to its economic potential. Most interviewees said that although they realize all countries are motivated by self-interest, the West has a moral duty to invest in community development for what one described as "the returns they have reaped from their investments in South Africa and the price of a foot in the door."

When questioned about the apparent contradiction between virulent criticism of the United States and the quest for additional American resources, a number of interviewees explained that attitudes toward the United States are shaped by two conflicting perceptions. On one level there is the negative perception of America's world role as an imperialist superpower, but there is also a very high regard for the priority the United States attaches to human rights. Thus blacks are essentially appealing to the United States to respond to their plight from a humanitarian motivation, and not only do they feel ideologically moved to condemn American global policy, but they are fearful that their own political ideals might be subverted by American political self-interest.

One interviewee aptly summed up the feeling of most others by saying, "We don't want to seem ungrateful, but it would be so much easier if American assistance was packaged so as not to affront black sensibilities." Thus, improving the American image among black South Africans depends not only on the reorientation of U.S. policy toward South Africa, but more fundamentally on a change in the characteristically patronizing attitude of many American visitors to South Africa toward black South Africans. One prominent community leader said she always got the impression that "Americans are on a mission to sell the American dream to the world." She added, "if only they would learn to navigate through local waters, people would accept their humane side much more readily."

There are a number of pointers to "navigating through local waters" that might facilitate American access to black community development.

The reason for getting involved: It is important for donors or prospective donors to be clear about the reasons for their interest in community development in South Africa. If the reason is primarily self-interest, such as assuaging divestment or withdrawal lobbyists, winning kudos from shareholders, quieting a restive student body, or building a political platform, then there is strong prospect of a hostile reception from black South Africans. If, on the other hand, the reason is primarily a humanitarian concern, there are a number of factors that will confirm the sincerity of this commitment in the eyes of black South Africans:

— be guided by the needs and aspirations of black South Africans;
— allow blacks to manage the initiative from the outset;
— address the basic causes of black disadvantage;
— make a long-term commitment;
— attempt to harness resources other than money, such as computer and agricultural equipment, training and technical expertise to ensure the effectiveness and long-term impact of the initiative.

Avoid the 'grand splash': One aspect of American involvement in community development in South Africa that is criticized most often is the pursuit of publicity. Photographs with the chairman of the board, the bronze plaque proclaiming patronage, the lengthy press releases and the often repeated public statements achieve some limited recognition among U.S. audiences, but are far outweighed by the damage to American credibility with black South Africans. The "grand splash" approach, as one interviewee put it, "leaves blacks cold."

The American penchant for public relations confirms black suspicions that Americans are motivated mostly by self-interest. A low-profile, no-publicity approach is much more likely to enjoy the cooperation of credible black leaders and organizations. Moreover, if the initiative is widely supported by black South Africans, then, as one interviewee noted, "the project will talk for itself."

'What have you to offer?': As indicated earlier, many black South Africans suspect that American concern is inherently shallow and, therefore, they initially are likely to be less than enthusiastic. Building trust and acceptance takes time and persistence. Acceptance largely comes when the donor shows a commitment to learn about South Africa from the black perspective. There is a fine line between what some interviewees perceived as contrived empathy and a sincere commitment to the future of South Africa.

Most interviewees referred disparagingly to the fact that many Americans make "lightning visits" to South Africa and base their perceptions upon "a trip to Soweto and tea with Tutu," as one put it. Interviewees confirmed that blacks generally find this attitude insulting and that the increasing number of such visits in recent months has been derisively dubbed "safari season" by some. A number of interviewees confirmed that they had decided to refuse appointments with visiting Americans, because they see them generally as a waste of time. One community worker bemoaned the fact that the droves of American visitors to South Africa are distracting busy, committed community leaders from their real task. She said, "Most people don't have the time to give repeated explanations of the South African problem."

On the other hand, those Americans who display a sincere commitment to learning about the situation and taking action to alleviate the plight of black South Africans will be warmly received. The essence of sincerity is a willingness to learn about South Africa from the black perspective, and to take one's direction from black South Africans from different walks of life — from Archbishop Tutu to factory workers and rural peasants. But as one interviewee counseled, "Always remember you are an American, and try as you may you will never be a black South African." He explained that blacks have had their fill of "soppy liberalism. . . . Sackcloth and ashes never got us anywhere. . . .We want action." The point is that if one has nothing to offer but sympathy, black South Africans are not likely to be enthusiastic.

Expect political flak: Because black South Africans are angered by U.S. policy toward South Africa, a measure of political flak is unavoidable. A number of interviewees mentioned that visiting Americans either spend a great deal of time defending the Reagan administration's policy or attempting to dissociate themselves from it. They noted that most Americans are very defensive about U.S. policy interests and, therefore, are bound to "pick up political flak."

The complexity of South African politics makes it difficult not to draw criticism from one quarter or another. However, interviewees counseled that one ought not to run away from political controversy. As one said, "It is important to establish the reasons for the blowout and to negotiate a way through it." Another interviewee said he thought "a test of wills is inevitable" where one has a "foreign interloper trying to do good and politically insecure people trying to resist being coopted."

The point is that Americans need to understand the nuances of the political situation in South Africa and be conscious of the fact that every action has a political connotation. What is perceived positively by one group might be denounced by another.

Do your homework: For the reasons discussed above and the fact that most black leaders have very demanding schedules, it is important that organizations and individuals without previous experience of South Africa do their homework before they go out to South Africa. Said one interviewee, "We can't start from scratch every time." There would be great benefit, he said, in targeting one's interest ahead of time and "doing a lot of spadework before hot-footing around South Africa."

Interviewees argued vigorously that critical black views should not be taken to mean that all projects should be abandoned. On the contrary, it was argued that awareness of the issues affecting black attitudes toward Americans would enhance the prospects for a mutually beneficial relationship. Despite the generally negative perceptions that most black leaders have of Americans, they are ready to allow those who approach the situation with sensitivity a chance to prove themselves. Moreover, as one interviewee put it, "South Africa is a society in turmoil. Much will be broken down, but that which blacks have adopted as their own will form the foundation of the new order."

IV.
RHETORIC
VERSUS REALITY:
WHAT OPPORTUNITIES
FOR AMERICAN
INVOLVEMENT?

The interviews that form the basis of this report are characterized by conflicting signals that alternately encourage and denigrate American involvement in community development in South Africa. These apparent contradictions cannot be dismissed entirely as emotional rhetoric because they are indeed symptomatic of deeper beliefs and fears. Unscrambling the signals is vital in understanding the limits as well as the opportunities for American involvement.

RHETORIC VERSUS REALITY

South Africa is in a state of violent political turmoil, and the range of potential outcomes can only be guessed at. However, it is clear that the foundation of a new order is being forged in the intense confrontation among different black and white groups. There are obviously a number of key actors in the process with conflicting objectives and perceptions of the end goal. Although no faction holds all the trumps to the final settlement, the South African government remains the most powerful. But black South Africans have acquired greater leverage over whites in recent years, principally through their sustained resistance to state repression, and also through their vital economic significance as skilled workers and consumers.

The political struggle in South Africa is aimed not only at ending white political domination. It is also about the sort of political regime that will replace the apartheid government and the redistribution of political power. Thus, black groups are themselves jockeying for political influence and the promise of power.

Moreover, normal political processes are inhibited by the imprisonment of key black political figures, the illegal status of the African National Congress and the Pan-Africanist Congress, and restrictions on public activities and financing of other political groups, such as the United Democratic Front. As a result, much of black politics inside South Africa is conducted surreptitiously, organizational links between leaders and supporters are relatively informal, and the level of mutual suspicion and personal acrimony among leaders and supporters of different groupings is high.

Furthermore, young blacks are increasingly disdainful of both non-violent channels of resistance and of established leadership. Thus, in order to retain a measure of credibility and influence with the more radical and impatient younger generation, the recognized black leadership cadre is itself forced to adopt an increasingly hard line. As one prominent black leader put it, "Everybody's power is negotiable all of the time."

The conflicting signals that characterize black South Africans' attitudes toward the United States are in part a reflection of this political turmoil, but there is also a deep suspicion among important sectors of the black community that the United States has imperialist designs on South Africa. The fear is that the United States will attempt to subvert the black liberation struggle and coopt the black leaders that best represent American interests. For black South Africans, the most striking evidence of American imperialism is U.S. support for Unita in Angola. Thus, they question how the United States can be trusted not to take advantage of factionalism within the black struggle in South Africa.

When political leaders are insecure and their constituencies divided, they tend to settle on issues on which all can agree. For black South Africans, vilification of the American policy of constructive engagement is common cause and has placed U.S. global policy and the role of Americans in South Africa in general in the spotlight of black political debate. The question is how much of the strident criticism of the United States and Americans can be discarded as rhetoric and how much represents a genuine ideological revulsion.

Part of the explanation is illustrated by the contradiction between the apparent hostility and simultaneous appeals for increasing American support for community development. This is largely a function of the conflicting perceptions that blacks have of the United States as an imperialist superpower on the one hand, and of the humanitarian commitment of Americans on the other. Although it is possible to make an intellectual distinction between the actions of the U.S. government and the American people, for the mass of black South Africans they are indistinguishable. Thus, the strong ideological revulsion and fear of American global imperialism colors black perceptions of all Americans.

On a different level, leading black South Africans have had considerable exposure to the large number of private American exploratory missions that have visited the country in recent years. These visits have not only raised expectations of far greater American assistance than has actually materialized, but have also underscored concerns that most Americans have preconceived perceptions of, and political goals for, South Africa that are generally at odds with those of black South Africans. Furthermore, much of the American money invested in community development, in the estimation of most of those interviewed, has been misdirected. As a result, many leading blacks are cynical about American intentions and are thus increasingly hostile toward Americans in general.

In addition, the harsh criticism leveled at the American business sector is a function of the deep frustration of black leadership at the political impotence and perceived political reticence of powerful American corporations. The high political profile adopted by American companies in South Africa awakened expectations in blacks of a much greater degree of socio-political activism by the American business sector and a belief that the corporations had more political clout than is in fact the case. These expectations have been disappointed.

Hostility toward the United States government has strong ideological roots and cannot be ascribed only to the legacy of constructive engagement. Furthermore, deep frustration with the seeming inability of Americans to deliver either material assistance or political pressure that matches black expectations and contributes to black goals underscores the widely articulated cynicism toward private American initiatives. The two levels of disenchantment are easily intertwined, and they contribute to the range of apparently conflicting signals reflected in this report.

Despite the ideological distaste with which blacks view the global activities of the United States, the reality is that there is no comparable alternative source of material assistance for community development. This fact is an additional source of discomfort and a major influence on the seemingly begrudging attitude toward American assistance.

However, black attitudes should not be construed as suggesting that American assistance is not needed or unwelcome. On the contrary, there is an unquenchable thirst for funds and assistance. The appeal is for an American approach that takes account of black political sensitivities and respects the right of black South Africans to determine their own priorities. Most importantly, blacks look to Americans for help in redressing the fundamental causes of black deprivation and preparing the ground for stable majority government.

OPPORTUNITIES FOR AMERICAN INVOLVEMENT

Clearly the uncertain political situation in South Africa obviates the viability of a conventional development approach to the problem of black deprivation and development. However, within the constraints outlined in this report, there are significant "pockets of opportunity" for American donors to make an impact on what blacks refer to as the "process of empowerment." Through carefully planned and well directed initiatives, it is possible to contribute to the development of institutions, leadership groups and processes that may be instrumental not only in accelerating the end of apartheid, but in preparing the ground for stable majority government.

This report has identified specific priorities for community development in South Africa, but the needs are so overwhelming and varied that it is difficult to give any one aspect precedence. Nevertheless, it is possible to identify a number of areas that provide the opportunity of initiating processes that could effect significant changes in the status quo that are crucial in the shaping of alternative systems.

An example is the potential ripple effect of well-designed rural subsistence schemes. Despite the constraints of land distribution and the need to skirt the homeland governments, providing rural communities with the skills of subsistence contributes to a greater sense of independence. In the process of community organization, rural communities become more familiar with bargaining and negotiating skills, which in turn gives them greater confidence in dealing with government authorities. A model for this kind of initiative is the Mboza Village project in the North Eastern parts of Natal, where the desperately impoverished rural community has organized educational, health and nutrition projects. Through the organizational skills acquired in the process of establishing the community projects, community leaders have acquired the confidence, experience and skills to be able to negotiate with state authorities for the release of irrigation water for the community's farming activities from a major storage dam nearby.

Furthermore, there are opportunities for the initiation of primary health care projects as part of a developing primary health care system that might in turn influence national health policy. One of the best models is the Ithuseng community health center at Tzaneen in the North Eastern Transvaal, which combines primary health care services with a nursery school, a community vegetable garden, a literacy program and a home industries workshop.

Perhaps the most promising possibilities for significant change in the status quo are in the area of education. The development of alternative education projects, such as Khanya College, will make a vital contribution to the redesigning of the South African education system and curricula. Similarly, the network of non-formal education programs is likely to prove more important than the discredited state-run system as the programs develop beyond remedial education to presenting alternative education within a formal curriculum. Already discussions are far advanced between non-formal education groups and the open universities on recognition of criteria other than the state school leaving certificate for university admission.

The granting of autonomy to the black universities presents the opportunity for significant change in the role that these institutions have played in black education to date. The University of the Western Cape has set the pace in attempting to reform the institution to reflect the goals and aspirations of blacks. Other black universities might be encouraged to follow this precedent. The key to this process is the development of academically competent black faculty and university administrators to take over from the whites who now control these institutions.

Although scholarships for study in the United States or at open universities in South Africa contribute significantly to the development of a skilled black professional cadre, most blacks do not qualify for a university education. Furthermore, the majority do not graduate from high school. This group is almost completely neglected in terms of overseas support, and attention should be given to "second chance education" programs, "distance learning" and other mid-career educational opportunities.

An obvious corollary to the demand for adult education is the need for training for manual and semi-skilled jobs to provide blacks with skills for "informal" income generation so as to facilitate the development of the "informal sector" as a potentially significant source of employment and income generation and thereby to lessen black dependence on the white-dominated industrial sector. Furthermore, attention should be given to the creation of business cooperatives and other income generating mechanisms aimed at placing greater wealth in the hands of blacks. The provision of venture capital for the development of small business enterprises would make a significant contribution to lessening black dependence for employment on the white-dominated industrial sector.

Further examples of opportunities for aiding the process of empowerment exist in the emerging network of advice offices and legal resources centers working to bring the due process of law in reach of the average black person and using it as an instrument of justice, rather than the instrument of oppression that it is wont to be. Similarly, the development of the emergent alternative media places an important instrument of self-expression in the hands of blacks, and this small pocket of freedom can be protected against state repression.

The most fundamental element in the process of "empowerment" through community development, however, is the nurturing of a network of black-run community organizations throughout the country. The development of such a network is important in facilitating the further expansion of community development efforts. The most crucial prerequisite is the training of an increasing cadre of individuals in the skills of community organization and institutional administration. Thus, this report has emphasized that priority should be given to training for community management.

Cynics would quite justifiably argue that none of this adds up to political liberation, and that without political equality community development projects simply wallpaper over the injustices of apartheid. However, as this report has documented, blacks see the external and internal liberation struggle as a continuum. Americans are in a powerful position to contribute to a process of "empowerment" that could ultimately enable blacks to liberate themselves. Whether American assistance is begrudgingly or willingly accepted depends entirely on the extent to which that assistance is guided by the aspirations, priorities and concerns of black South Africans.

APPENDIX I

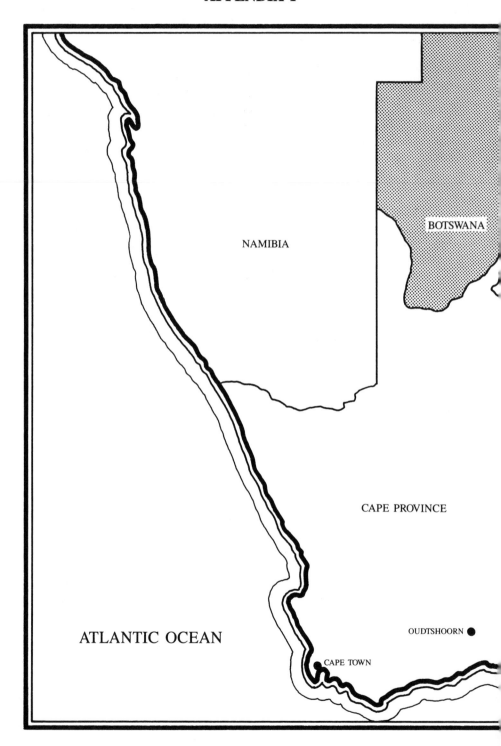

SOUTHERN AFRICA

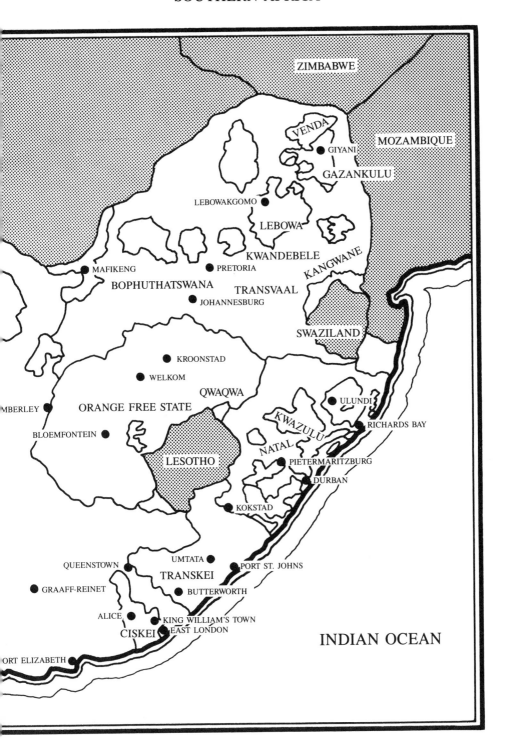

ZIMBABWE

MOZAMBIQUE

VENDA

GIYANI

GAZANKULU

LEBOWAKGOMO

LEBOWA

KWANDEBELE

KANGWANE

MAFIKENG

PRETORIA

BOPHUTHATSWANA

TRANSVAAL

JOHANNESBURG

SWAZILAND

KROONSTAD

WELKOM

QWAQWA

ULUNDI

MBERLEY

ORANGE FREE STATE

RICHARDS BAY

BLOEMFONTEIN

KWAZULU

NATAL

LESOTHO

PIETERMARITZBURG

DURBAN

KOKSTAD

UMTATA

PORT ST. JOHNS

QUEENSTOWN

TRANSKEI

GRAAFF-REINET

BUTTERWORTH

ALICE

KING WILLIAM'S TOWN

CISKEI

EAST LONDON

ORT ELIZABETH

INDIAN OCEAN

THE FREEDOM CHARTER

PREAMBLE

We, the people of South Africa, declare for all our country and the world to know: —
That South Africa belongs to all who live in it, black and white, and that no government can justly claim authority unless it is based on the will of the people;
That our people have been robbed of their birthright to land, liberty and peace by a form of government founded on injustice and inequality;
That our country will never be prosperous or free until all our people live in brotherhood, enjoying equal rights and opportunities;
That only a democratic state, based on the will of the people can secure to all their birthright without distinction of colour, race, sex or belief;
And therefore, we, the people of South Africa, black and white, together — equals, countrymen and brothers — adopt this FREEDOM CHARTER. And we pledge ourselves to strive together, sparing nothing of our strength and courage, until the democratic changes here set out have been won.

THE PEOPLE SHALL GOVERN

Every man and woman shall have the right to vote for and stand as a candidate for all bodies which make laws.
All the people shall be entitled to take part in the administration of the country.
The rights of the people shall be the same regardless of race, colour or sex.
All bodies of minority rule, advisory boards, councils and authorities shall be replaced by democratic organs of self-government.

ALL NATIONAL GROUPS SHALL HAVE EQUAL RIGHTS

There shall be equal status in the bodies of state, in the courts and in the schools for all national groups and races;
All national groups shall be protected by law against insults to their race and national pride;

All people shall have equal rights to use their own language and to develop their own folk culture and customs;

The preaching and practice of national, race or colour discrimination and contempt shall be a punishable crime;

All apartheid laws and practices shall be set aside.

THE PEOPLE SHALL SHARE IN THE COUNTRY'S WEALTH

The national wealth of our country, the heritage of all South Africans, shall be restored to the people;

The mineral wealth beneath the soil, the banks and monopoly industry shall be transferred to the ownership of the people as a whole;

All other industries and trade shall be controlled to assist the well-being of the people;

All people shall have equal rights to trade where they choose, to manufacture and to enter all trades, crafts and professions.

THE LAND SHALL BE SHARED AMONG THOSE WHO WORK IT

Restriction of land ownership on a racial basis shall be ended, and all the land re-divided amongst those who work it, to banish famine and land hunger;

The state shall help the peasants with implements, seed, tractors and dams to save the soil and assist the tillers;

Freedom of movement shall be guaranteed to all who work on the land;

All shall have the right to occupy land wherever they choose;

People shall not be robbed of their cattle; forced labour and farm prisons shall be abolished.

ALL PEOPLE SHALL BE EQUAL BEFORE THE LAW

No one shall be imprisoned, deported or restricted without a fair trial;

No one shall be condemned by the order of any Government official;

The courts shall be representative of all the people;

Imprisonment shall be only for serious crimes against the people, and shall aim at re-education, not vengeance;

The police force and army shall be open to all on an equal basis and shall be the helpers and protectors of the people;

All laws which discriminate on grounds of race, colour or belief shall be repealed.

ALL SHALL ENJOY EQUAL HUMAN RIGHTS

The law shall guarantee to all their right to speak, to organise, to meet together, to publish, to preach, to worship and to educate their children;

The privacy of the house from police raids shall be protected by law;

All shall be free to travel without restriction from countryside to town, from province to province, and from South Africa abroad;

Pass laws, permits and all other laws restricting these freedoms shall be abolished.

THERE SHALL BE WORK AND SECURITY

All who work shall be free to form trade unions, to elect their officers and to make wage agreements with their employers;

The state shall recognise the right and duty of all to work, and to draw full unemployment benefits;

Men and women of all races shall receive equal pay for equal work;

There shall be a forty-hour working week, a national minimum wage, paid annual leave, and sick leave for all workers, and maternity leave on full pay for all working mothers;

Miners, domestic workers, farm workers and civil servants shall have the same rights as all others who work;

Child labor, compound labour, the tot system and contract labour shall be abolished.

THE DOORS OF LEARNING AND OF CULTURE SHALL BE OPENED

The government shall discover, develop and encourage national talent for the enhancement of our cultural life;

All the cultural treasures of mankind shall be open to all, by free exchange of books, ideas and contacts with other lands;

The aim of education shall be to teach the youth to love their people and their culture, to honour human brotherhood, liberty and peace;

Education shall be free, compulsory, universal and equal for all children;

Higher education and technical training shall be opened to all by means of state allowances and scholarships awarded on the basis of merit;

Adult illiteracy shall be ended by a mass state education plan;

Teachers shall have all the rights of other citizens;

The colour bar in cultural life, in sport and in education shall be abolished.

THERE SHALL BE HOUSES, SECURITY AND COMFORT

All people shall have the right to live where they choose, to be decently housed, and to bring up their families in comfort and security;

Unused housing space to be available to the people;

Rent and prices shall be lowered, food plentiful and no one shall go hungry;

A preventive health scheme shall be run by the state;

Free medical care and hospitalisation shall be provided for all, with special care for mothers and young children;

Slums shall be demolished and new suburbs built where all have transport, roads, lighting, playing fields, creches and social centres;

The aged, the orphans, the disabled and the sick shall be cared for by the state;

Rest, leisure and recreation shall be the right of all;

Fenced locations and ghettoes shall be abolished, and laws which break up families shall be repealed.

THERE SHALL BE PEACE AND FRIENDSHIP

South Africa shall be a fully independent state, which respects the rights and sovereignty of all nations;

South Africa shall strive to maintain world peace and the settlement of all international disputes by negotiation — not war;

Peace and friendship amongst all our people shall be secured by upholding the equal rights, opportunities and status of all;

The people of the protectorates — Basutoland, Bechuanaland and Swaziland — shall be free to decide for themselves their own future;

The right of all the peoples of Africa to independence and self-government shall be recognised, and shall be the basis of close cooperation.

LET ALL WHO LOVE THEIR PEOPLE AND THEIR COUNTRY NOW SAY, AS WE SAY HERE:
"THESE FREEDOMS WE WILL FIGHT FOR, SIDE BY SIDE, THROUGHOUT OUR LIVES, UNTIL WE HAVE WON OUR LIBERTY."

MANIFESTO OF THE AZANIAN PEOPLE

Our struggle for national liberation is directed against the historically evolved system of racism and capitalism which holds the people of Azania in bondage for the benefit of the small minority of the population, i.e. the capitalists and their allies, the white workers and the reactionary sections of the middle classes. The struggle against apartheid, therefore, is no more than the point of departure for our liberatory efforts.

The Black working class inspired by revolutionary consciousness is the driving force of our struggle for national self determination in a unitary Azania. They alone can end the system as it stands today because they alone have nothing at all to lose. They have a world to gain in a democratic, anti-racist and socialist Azania, where the interests of the workers shall be paramount through worker control of the means of production, distribution and exchange. In the socialist republic of Azania the land and all that belongs to it shall be wholly owned and controlled by the Azanian people. The usage of the land and all that accrues to it shall be aimed at ending all exploitation.

It is the historic task of the Black working class and its organizations to mobilise the oppressed and exploited people in order to put an end to the system of oppression and exploitation by the white ruling class.

OUR PRINCIPLES

Successful conduct of the national liberation struggle depends on the firm basis of principles whereby we will ensure that the liberation struggle will not be turned against our people by treacherous and opportunistic "leaders" and liberal influences. The most important of these principles are:

Anti-racism, anti-imperialism and anti-sexism.

Anti-collaboration with the ruling class and
all its allies and political instruments.

Independent working class organization,
free from bourgeois influences.

OUR RIGHTS

In accordance with these principles the following rights shall be entrenched in Azania:

The right to work.

State provision of free and compulsory education for all. Education shall be geared towards liberating the Azanian people from all oppression, exploitation and ignorance.

State provision of adequate and decent housing.

State provision of free health, legal, recreational, and other community services that will respond positively to the needs of the people.

OUR PLEDGES

In order to bring into effect these rights of the Azanian people, we pledge ourselves to struggle tirelessly for:

The abolition of all laws, institutions and attitudes that discriminate against our people on the basis of colour, sex, religion, language or class.

The re-integration of the bantustan human dumping grounds into a unitary Azania.

The formation of trade unions that will heighten revolutionary worker consciousness.

The development of one national culture inspired by socialist values.

DIRECTORY

The following is a directory of organizations referred to in the text of this report. This is not an exhaustive list of organizations that might be supported by American donors, but a guide to key institutions that will facilitate access to the community development network in South Africa.

The reference at the foot of each entry is to the subject area and page in the text of the report.

ADDRESS	CONTACT PERSON	TELEPHONE
Adopt-a-School Box 47152 Parklands 2121 Johannesburg	Cynthia Hugo	(011)788-6833

REFERENCE: black school facilities, p. 35

Advice Centers' Association (ACA) Suite 201, 2nd Floor Union Centre 31 Pritchard Street Johannesburg 2001	Pule Pule	(011)838-2593

REFERENCE: legal representation, p. 47

African National Congress (ANC) 801 2nd Avenue New York, N.Y. 10017	Neo Numzama	(212)490-3487
Box 31791 Lusaka, Zambia	Lindelwe Mbandla	(Lusaka) 219-657

REFERENCE: black politics, p. 4

African Teachers' Association of South Africa (Atasa) Box 90064 Bertsham 2103 Johannesburg	Randall Petini	(011)933-1093

REFERENCE: intermediary organization, p. 53

ADDRESS	CONTACT PERSON	TELEPHONE

American Chamber of
Commerce in South
Africa (Amcham)
60 5th Street
Lower Houghton 2196
Johannesburg

Ken Mason

(011)788-0265

REFERENCE: U.S. business association, p. 34

Azanian Congress of
Trade Unions (Azactu)
2nd Floor, Abbey House
51 Commissioner Street
Johannesburg 2001

P. Nefolafodwe
Letsatsi Mosala

(011)843-6682

REFERENCE: black trade union, p. 10

Azanian People's
Organization (Azapo)
Box 4230
Johannesburg 2000

George Wauchope

(011)230-013
230-112

REFERENCE: black politics, p. 6

Bishop Desmond Tutu
Southern Africa Refugee
  Scholarship Fund
c/o Phelps Stokes Fund
  10 East 87th Street
  New York, N.Y. 10017

Bernice Powell

(212)427-8100

REFERENCE: refugee programs, p. 49

Black Housewives' League
1401/2 Ntipa Street
P.O. Dube 1852
Soweto

Sally Motlana

(011)930-1312

REFERENCE: subsistence agriculture, p. 26

ADDRESS	CONTACT PERSON	TELEPHONE
Black Lawyers' Association (BLA) Box 61246 Marshalltown 2107 Johannesburg	Godfrey Pitje	(011)337-1536

REFERENCE: intermediary organization, p. 48

Black Legal Education Center Box 4118 Johannesburg 2000	Modise Khoza	(011)337-1536

REFERENCE: legal representation, p. 48

Black Management Forum (BMF) Box 11499 Johannesburg 2000	Eric Mafuna Ernest Mcunu	(011)331-6254 339-4856

REFERENCE: intermediary organization, p. 51

Black Sash Khotso House 42 de Villiers Street Johannesburg 2000	Sheena Duncan	(011)337-2435

REFERENCE: victims of apartheid, p. 47

Careers Research and Information Center (Cric) Box 78 Claremont 7735	Trish Fliederman	(021)611-058

REFERENCE: career guidance, p. 35

Center for Applied Legal Studies (Cals) 1 Jan Smuts Avenue Braamfontein 2001 Johannesburg	Prof. John Dugard	(011)716-1111

REFERENCE: legal representation, p. 48

ADDRESS	CONTACT PERSON	TELEPHONE
Center for Social Development Box 94 Grahamstown 6140	Thelma Henderson	(0461)4483

REFERENCE: pre-school education, p. 32

| Community Resource
and Information Center (Cric)
Box 16105
Doornfontein 2028
Johannesburg | Auret van Heerden | (011)339-2139 |

REFERENCE: community leader development, p. 51

| Congress of South African
Trade Unions (Cosatu)
Box 1019
Johannesburg 2000 | Jay Naidoo
Sydney Mafumadi | (011)402-2330 |

REFERENCE: black trade union, p. 9

| Council of Unions of
South Africa (Cusa)
Box 10928
Johannesburg 2000 | Piroshaw Camay
Dale Tifflin | (011)298-031 |

REFERENCE: black trade union, p. 10

| Detainees Parents Support
Committee (DPSC)
Box 92
Johannesburg 2000 | Max Coleman | (011)23666/4/5 |

| Box 39431
Bramley 2018 | | (011)646-9904 |

REFERENCE: legal representation, p. 48

| Diakonia
Box 1879
Durban 4000 | Paddy Kearney | (031)312-609 |

REFERENCE: intermediary organization, p. 53

ADDRESS	CONTACT PERSON	TELEPHONE

Early Learning   Anne Short   (021)679-146
Resource Unit
Springbok Street
Kewtown, Athlone 7764
Cape Town

REFERENCE: pre-school education, p. 32

Education Information Center   Marion MacNair   (011)339-2476
(EIC)
Dunwell House
35 Jorissen Street
Braamfontein 2007

REFERENCE: career guidance, p. 35

Educational Opportunities   Dr. Mokgethi Mothlabi   (011)833-1510
Council (EOC)
Box 31190
Braamfontein 2017

REFERENCE: scholarships, p. 40

Entokozweni Early Learning   Mapitso Malepo   (011)930-3711
and Community Center
Box 54
KwaXuma 1868

REFERENCE: pre-school education, p. 32

Freedom Charter   Dumi Mathabane   (301)350-4323
Education Fund
6804 Wilburn Drive
Capitol Heights, Md. 20743

REFERENCE: refugee programs, p. 49

Funda Center   Stan Khan   (011)933-2421
Box 359   Prof. Zeke Mpahlele   (011)716-1111
Orlando 1804
Soweto

REFERENCE: alternative education, p. 46

ADDRESS	CONTACT PERSON	TELEPHONE

Get Ahead Foundation
Box 3776
Pretoria 0001

Don Macrobert

(012)346-1070

REFERENCE: small business development, p. 45

Grassroots
1st Floor
10 Corporation Street
Cape Town 8000

Saleem Badat

(021)452-325

REFERENCE: alternative media, p. 50

Grassroots Education Trust
Industria House
350 Victoria Road
Salt River 7925
Cape Town

Jinny Richards

(021)472-546

REFERENCE: pre-school education, p. 32

Health Services Development
Unit (HSDU)
Medical School
York Road
Parktown 2193
Johannesburg

Cedric de Beer

(011)647-1111

REFERENCE: primary health care, p. 31

Health Workers' Association
Box 38266
Booysens 2014
Johannesburg

Rafik Bismillah

(011)852-7677

REFERENCE: health care, intermediary organization, p. 30

Independent Mediation Services
of South Africa (IMSSA)
Box 91082
Auckland Park 2006
Johannesburg

Julian Riekert

(011)726-7104

REFERENCE: black labor union development, p. 51

ADDRESS	CONTACT PERSON	TELEPHONE

Industrial Aid Society   George Moila   (011)238-467
Box 261119
Excom 2023
Johannesburg

REFERENCE: black labor union development, p. 51

Inkatha   Dr. Oscar Dlhomo   (0358)74-2016
Private Bag X01   74-933
Ulundi 3838

Box 82   Zora Khumalo   (011)920-2702
Tembisa 1628

REFERENCE: black politics, p. 10

Institute for Social   Prof. Peter Vale   (0461)22023
and Economic Research
Box 94
Grahamstown 6140

REFERENCE: policy skills training, p. 43

Interchurch Media Program   Rev. Bernard Spong   (011)726-7969
Box 9942
Johannesburg 2000

REFERENCE: alternative media, p. 50

Inter-denominational African   Rev. De Villiers Sogo   (041)441-328
Ministers' Association   Patrick Pasha   392-040
of South Africa (Idamasa)
Box 7051
Newton Park 6055
Port Elizabeth

REFERENCE: intermediary organization, p. 53

ADDRESS	CONTACT PERSON	TELEPHONE
Khanya College 31 Pritchard Street Johannesburg 2000	Glen Fisher	(011)836-331
Park Fair Building Trematon Street Athlone 7764 Cape Town	Eilene Meyer	(021)668-507

REFERENCE: post-secondary education, p. 33

Lawyers for Human Rights Box 7613 Johannesburg 2000	The Secretary	(011)231-210

REFERENCE: legal representation, p. 48

Learn and Teach Magazine 3rd Floor Merlen House 49 Simmonds Street Johannesburg 2001	Temba Mkwanazi	(011)834-4011

REFERENCE: alternative media, p. 50

Legal Resources Center (LRC) Box 9495 Johannesburg 2000	Arthur Chaskelson Geoff Budlender	(011)836-9831

REFERENCE: legal representation, p. 48

Mboza Village Project c/o African Studies Dept. Univ. of Natal King George V Avenue Durban 4000	Peter Derman	(031)816-9111

REFERENCE: rural subsistence, p. 72

Media and Resource Service Freeway House 9 de Korte Street Braamfontein 2001 Johannesburg	Carl Becker	(011)339-2139

REFERENCE: alternative media, p. 50

ADDRESS	CONTACT PERSON	TELEPHONE
Media Workers' Association (MWASA) Box 6663 Johannesburg 2000	Thami Mazwai Joe Thloloe	(011)673-4160

REFERENCE: leadership groups, p. 51

Medical Education for South African Blacks (Mesab) 1011 North Capitol Street N.E. Washington D.C. 20002	Herb Kaiser	(202)898-5375

REFERENCE: medical training, p. 31

Medical University of South Africa (Medunsa) P.O. Medunsa 0204	Prof. L.C. Taljaard	(012)582844

REFERENCE: medical training, p. 28

National African Federated Chamber of Commerce (Nafcoc) Box 220 Ga-Rankuwa 0208	Sam Motsuenyane Stan Khubekha	(01214)2024

REFERENCE: intermediary organization, p. 53

National Education Crisis Committee (NECC) Suite 206, Darragh House Cnr. Plein and Wanderers Street Johannesburg 2001	Vusi Khanyile Rev. J. Tsele	(021)694-351 (011)291-478

REFERENCE: education/intermediary organization, p. 32

National Medical and Dental Association (Namda) Box 16108 Randfontein 2028 Johannesburg	Wendy Cullinan	(011)726-2007

REFERENCE: intermediary organization, p. 30

ADDRESS	CONTACT PERSON	TELEPHONE
New Era Schools Trust (Nest) 28 St. Patrick's Road Houghton 2193 Johannesburg	Dean Yates	(011)648-4327

REFERENCE: non-racial private schools, p. 34

New Nation Box 32549 Braamfontein 2017 Johannesburg	Zwelakhe Sisulu	(011)232-711

REFERENCE: alternative media, p. 50

Operation Hunger Box 97 Johannesburg 2000	Ina Perlman	(011)339-2381

REFERENCE: famine relief, p. 26

Pace College Pvt. Bag X11 Kwa-Xuma 1868 Soweto	The Headmaster	(011)930-3541

REFERENCE: black private school, p. 34

Pan-Africanist Congress (PAC) 211 East 43rd Street New York, N.Y. 10017	Count Pietersen	(212)986-7378

REFERENCE: black politics, p. 4

Read Box 47152 Parklands 2121 Johannesburg	Cynthia Hugo	(011)788-6833

REFERENCE: black literacy, p. 36

Rhodes University Box 94 Grahamstown 6140	Dr. Derrick Henderson	(0461)22023

REFERENCE: "open university," p. 38

ADDRESS	CONTACT PERSON	TELEPHONE

Rural Fulfillment Foundation
Box 645
Constantia 7848
Cape Town

Phil Clinton

(021)744-284

REFERENCE: subsistence agriculture, p. 27

Self-Help Associates for
Development Economics
(Shade)
Box 81
Roodepoort 1725

Carl Keyter

(011)763-2650

REFERENCE: subsistence agriculture, p. 26

Signatory Association
Box 9773
Johannesburg 2000

Lionel Grewan

(011)833-5763

REFERENCE: U.S. business organization, p. 63

Skotaville Publishers
Box 32483
Braamfontein 2017
Johannesburg

Mothobi Mutloatse

(011)339-1874

REFERENCE: alternative media, p. 50

Small Business Development
Corporation (SBDC)
Box 4300
Johannesburg 2000

Ben Vosloo

(011)643-7531

REFERENCE: small business development, p. 45

Solomon Mahlangu Freedom
College (Somafco)
Private Bag Mazimbu
P.O. Morogoro
Tanzania

Marius Schoon

(Morogoro)2257

REFERENCE: refugee programs, p. 49

ADDRESS	CONTACT PERSON	TELEPHONE
South African Black Social Workers' Association (Sabswa) Box 54503 Umlazi 4031	Felix Dhlamini	(031)425-121

REFERENCE: intermediary organization, p. 53

South African Committee for Higher Education (Sached) Box 11350 Johannesburg 2000	John Samuel	(011)834-1341
5 Church Street Mowbray 7700 Cape Town	Dr. Neville Alexander	(021)668-615

REFERENCE: alternative education, p. 33

South African Council of Churches (SACC) Box 31190 Braamfontein 2017 Johannesburg	Rev. Beyers Naude	(011)282-251

REFERENCE: intermediary organization, p. 16

South African Education Program (SAEP) 809 UN Plaza First Avenue New York N.Y. 10017	Sheila McLean	(212)883-8200

REFERENCE: scholarships, p. 40

South African Institute of Race Relations (SAIRR) Box 97 Johannesburg 2000	John Kane-Berman Sylvia Gon	(011)724-4441

REFERENCE: scholarships, p. 40

South African Red Cross Box 8726 Johannesburg 2000	Rosa Ferreira	(011)292-4490

REFERENCE: refugee and famine relief programs, p. 26

ADDRESS	CONTACT PERSON	TELEPHONE
Southern Africa Legal Services and Education Project (Salslep) 2445 M Street N.W. Washington D.C. 20037-1420	Reuben Clark	(202)663-6000

REFERENCE: legal assistance, p. 48

Southern African Catholic Bishops' Conference Box 941 Pretoria 0001	Rev. Smangaliso Mkhatshwa	(012)323-6458

REFERENCE: intermediary organization, p. 16

Southern African Training Program c/o African-American Institute 833 UN Plaza New York, N.Y. 10017	Susan Anderson	(212)949-5666

REFERENCE: refugee programs, p. 49

Soweto Career Center Box 38 Orlando 1804 Soweto	Sebelelo Mohajane	(011)938-1439

REFERENCE: career guidance, p. 35

Soweto Civic Association Box 164 Orlando 1804 Soweto	Ntatho Motlana	(011)939-4039 (011)933-1929

REFERENCE: black politics, p. 16

Speak Box 261677 Excom 2023 Johannesburg	Feizel Mamdoo	(011)339-3975 339-6354

REFERENCE: alternative media, p. 50

ADDRESS	CONTACT PERSON	TELEPHONE
St. Barnabas College Box 88188 Newclare 2112	Michael Corke	(011)673-6741
St. Barnabas College Fund 230 Park Avenue New York, N.Y. 10169	Hubert Mandeville	(212)986-3377

REFERENCE: black private school, p. 34

Students' Health and Welfare Centers (Shawco) 12th Avenue Kensington 7405 Cape Town	David Livisey	(021)516-147

REFERENCE: community health programs, p. 31

Teachers' Opportunities Program (TOPS) Private Bag 682 Johannesburg 2000	Gerard Murphy	(011)292-321

REFERENCE: teacher upgrading, p. 36

Technical Advice Group (TAG) Box 32358 Braamfontein 2017 Johannesburg	Rina King	(011)339-1340

REFERENCE: black labor union development, p. 51

Trust for Christian Outreach and Education Box 2283 Pietermaritzburg 3200	Rev. Bennie Witbooi	(0331)81291

REFERENCE: intermediary organization, p. 31

ADDRESS	CONTACT PERSON	TELEPHONE
United Democratic Front (UDF) Box 10366 Johannesburg 2000	Azhar Cachalia	(011)291-916
7372 Orlando West P.O. Orlando Soweto 1804	Albertina Sisulu	(011)939-4332
6 Hoek Street Glenhaven 7533 Cape Town	Rev. Allan Boesak	(021)952-763

REFERENCE: black politics, p. 6

United States-South Africa Leader Exchange Program (USSALEP) Box 23053 Joubert Park 2044 Johannesburg	Hazel Moolman	(011)339-6774
1700 17th Street N.W. Washington D.C. 20009	Mariella Lehfeldt	(202)232-6720

REFERENCE: community leader development, p. 51

United Workers' Union of South Africa (UWUSA) 4th Floor, Salisbury Center Tower C West Street Durban 4001	Simon Conco	(031)304-9691

REFERENCE: black trade union, p. 10

Univ. of Bophuthatswana Pvt. Bag X2046 Mafikeng Bophuthatswana	Prof. John Moklere	(01401)21171

REFERENCE: black university, p. 38

ADDRESS	CONTACT PERSON	TELEPHONE
Univ. of Cape Town P.O. Rondebosch 7700 Cape Town	James Moulder	(021)698–531
Univ. of Cape Town Fund Inc. 135 East 65th Street New York, N.Y. 10021	Anne Moran	(212)754-8970

REFERENCE: "open university," p. 38

Univ. of Durban-Westville Private Bag X54001 Durban 4000	Prof. J.C. Greyling	(031)820-9111

REFERENCE: black university, p. 38

Univ. of Fort Hare Pvt. Bag X1314 Alice 5700 Republic of Ciskei	Prof. J.A. Lamprecht	(Alice)370-455

REFERENCE: black university, p. 38

Univ. of Natal King George V Avenue Durban 4001	Prof. P. de V. Booysen	(031)816-9111

REFERENCE: "open university," p. 38

Univ. of the North (Turfloop) Pvt. Bag X1090 Sovenga 0700	John Malatji	(01522)4310

REFERENCE: black university, p. 38

Univ. of the Western Cape Private Bag X17 Bellville 7530	Prof. Jakes Gerwel	(021)951-4101
Good Hope Foundation 425 Ninita Parkway Pasadena, Calif. 91106	Prof. Ned Munger	(818)356-4468

REFERENCE: black university, p. 38

ADDRESS	CONTACT PERSON	TELEPHONE
Univ. of the Witwatersrand 1 Jan Smuts Avenue Braamfontein 2001 Johannesburg	Prof. Mervyn Shear	(011)716-1111

REFERENCE: "open university," p. 38

Univ. of Zululand Pvt. Bag X1001 Kwa-Dlangweza 3886 Kwa Zulu	Prof. A. Nkabinde	(0351)93911
Univ. of Zululand Foundation 420 Lexington Avenue New York, N.Y. 10170	Rich Hilser	(212)867-0616

REFERENCE: black university, p. 38

University Preparation Program (UPP) 6th Floor, 34 Ameshof Road Braamfontein Johannesburg 2001	Fanyana Mazibuko	(011)339-1655

REFERENCE: remedial and alternative education, p. 33

Urban Foundation Box 1198 Johannesburg 2000	Deborah Mabiletsa Musi Myeni	(011)833-1620
c/o Murden & Co. 477 Madison Avenue New York, N.Y. 10022	Charles Muller	(212)752-6515

REFERENCE: housing, p. 45

Urban Training Project (UTP) Box 25271 Ferreirasdorp 2048 Johannesburg	Reuben Denge	(011)838-2181

REFERENCE: black labor union development, p. 51

ADDRESS	CONTACT PERSON	TELEPHONE
Valley Trust Box 33 Botha's Hill 3660	Friedman Mann	(031)777–1955

REFERENCE: subsistence agriculture, p. 26

Western Cape Foundation for Community Work Springbok Street Kewtown, Athlone 7764	Beryl Baatjes	(021)679-148

REFERENCE: pre-school education, p. 32

Wilgespruit Fellowship Center Box 81 Roodepoort 1725	Rev. Dale White	(011)763-1270

REFERENCE: community leader development, p. 51

World Vision 5 Main Avenue Florida 1710 Johannesburg	John Allwood	(011)674-2043
220 I Street N.E. Washington D.C. 20002	Tom Getman	(202)547-3743

REFERENCE: relief programs, p. 26